SHE'S *Still* STANDING

A Journey of Transformation

By
ELAINE M. GRANT

xulon PRESS

Dedication

T hanks to God first, as He has proven Himself to be a Father, Friend and most importantly my Saviour, and Deliverer. I would not be alive today if you had not extended your love, mercy, and grace unto me. I would not want to live this life without You. My love for You, runs deep, and overflows. You are everything to me. All the glory belongs to You!

To my parents, Olive Grant and Albert Grant (deceased), thank you for doing your very best to take care of me and imparting unto me good moral values to live by. God does not make a mistake with whom he chooses to use as vessels to bring us into the world. I am grateful He chose you both.

To my daughter Tasia Casandra Brown, throughout the years I have always felt we were growing up together. You have had a front row seat to my transformation. Thank you for your love and support along the way. You are my daughter, sister, and friend.

To my loved ones, thank you for your love, support and encouragement. All of you have added some dynamic to my life. I am blessed. You are the best family.

To my editorial assistants, Tasia Casandra Brown, Ruth Fisher, Yvonne Asary-Aboagye, Diana Gimba and Patricia Braithwaite. Thank you for sacrificing your time. I appreciate your labour of love. God bless you.

To all those who have given words of encouragement to write my story, you know who you are. I say thank you.

To my Pastors, Dr. Ralph Dartey and Pastor Regina Dartey (Transforming Life Centre), I thank you for your spiritual covering. May God continue to bless you as you work in His vineyard transforming lives and raising leaders.

Finally, this book is dedicated to all those who have found themselves in a dark place. Those who are struggling with some form of addiction, and have felt out of place in this world. I know that there is help for you; there is deliverance from a loving God that is very real. He did it for me and He will do the same for you.

Contents

Introduction ix

1. The Early Years 11
2. Runaway 43
3. Working Girl. 47
4. The Club Life 85
5. Changes 111
6. The Normal Life. 125
7. Hitting Bottom 191
8. Jesus Heard Me .223
9. Starting Over. 243
10. Church Life. 261
11. The Refiner's Fire. 275
12. A New Story 313

Introduction

O ur lives are made up of a number of factors, events and moments that shape and mould your character, behaviour, thoughts and emotions.

Writing this book was an eye opener for me. It gave me a full understanding of certain experiences in my life and allowed me to have clarity and a better perspective of myself.

I now understand that my life has been shaped significantly by all of my experiences; the most important was making Jesus the head and centre of my life. I am experiencing His freedom, living a new life. I recognize how many of my experiences happened for a reason. Now I know I am heading in the right direction.

I am in a very exciting time of my life and I am ready for a new chapter. This could not have happened until I was able to reflect over the life I have lived.

My hope is that by sharing my story, it will help you to reflect over your own life. If you have ever felt overwhelmed by life, taken a back seat, struggled with self-esteem, self-confidence and any form of addiction (whether alcohol, drugs, sexual, food etc.) or if you feel you do not belong in this world, this book is for you. I hope by the end of this story you will recognize, as I did, that everything you have been through, or are going through, is a part of your journey and if you allow Jesus to help, He will see you through until the end. It is never too late.

By the end of this book, I hope you can see yourself achieving the desires of your heart and seeing God's heart for you. You can persevere and achieve your goals. You can get in touch and connected with your inner creativity.

If you will allow Him to lead, you can't go wrong; you cannot lose, but you will come out a winner.

CHAPTER ONE

The Early Years

My name is Elaine. This is my story. This is my truth.

When I was a little girl enjoying life in Jamaica, I didn't know as I grew up that the events in my life would lead me into the darkest of places. I would have to learn what it meant to endure and overcome many obstacles, and challenges while experiencing the most difficult of times. Some of these challenges would cause me to travel down a path of drinking, drugs, and promiscuity.

Looking back over my life I cannot come to any other conclusion, than that the odds were stacked up against me. It's a miracle I am alive.

My land of birth is the beautiful island of Jamaica. I only spent ten years of my life there, yet it had a lasting impact on me.

My earliest memory of Jamaica was being at my parents wedding. I was about six years of age. I remember that it was a rainy day. Everyone was so happy, and joyful. The next day at my Grandma's house, my sister Deirdre and I had a lot of fun helping our parents open their many wedding gifts given by family and friends. Still celebrating, I went along with Momma to hand out slices of wedding cake to our surrounding neighbours. We had such fun as a family, along with close family friends. I remember those nights when we would all be on Grandma's veranda, the music would be blasting and the neighbours would come by and hang out.

My parents were both hard workers. They were always doing whatever it took to give their children a better life; therefore it was a great day when Momma was given an opportunity to go to Canada to work. Before Momma left for Canada, it was decided that my older brother Kendal would stay in Kingston to live with Grandma. Deirdre and

I were brought to the country and put in the trust and care of my father's youngest sister, Aunt Pat. My other Aunt Florence and Uncle Kenneth lived on the adjoining land. An older boy name Simon, and a much older girl Patty were also left in her care. Aunt Pat took care of us all by herself; her husband had passed away years before. While our parents were working to give us a better life, I learned a lot watching Aunt Pat. She was devoted to the church we attended, and to her position as a church leader. She was strict, making sure all of us stayed out of trouble. When Aunt Pat went to church we went to church. Sometimes we were at church for what seemed like all day, going home for a few hours, then back again later in the evening late into the night. I enjoyed going to church. I remember a pair of sisters; they were in their late teens or early twenties. One of the sisters was a favourite of mine; I loved the way she was so skilful at playing the tambourine. When I got my hands on one, I would try and imitate her.

With Momma away in Canada, Daddy was still in Jamaica working hard. Daddy came to visit us often. I always looked forward to when Daddy would come; you never knew what he would bring when he showed up. It could be a drum barrel full of crabs or it could be two ducks, one each for Deirdre and I, to have as pets. They were beautiful white ducks. One time Momma sent Deirdre and I dolls from Canada. They were big and pretty. Deirdre's doll could walk and talk, which was exciting to see since we had never seen a doll do that before. On one of Daddy's visits we told him we didn't have beds for our dolls. What did Daddy do? He came back on his next visit with two beds made for both our dolls. We were very happy. I'm not sure who made them, but they fit our dolls perfectly.

The few years spent with Aunt Pat and the rest of our family were fun years for me as a child. It seemed as if the sky was so close to the ground, where we lived. I remember thinking that God was so close, especially when it rained and there was lightening and thunder. I heard that God and the devil were fighting when there was lighting and thunder, or the devil and his wife. I actually believed it.

There were a lot of kids to play with, including our cousins. We would catch bees and place them in bottles. To catch the bees we used finger protectors made out of paper, so as not to get stung by them. We always set them free later. The butterflies were much harder to catch.

Crab season was a lot of fun. We would get up early in the morning on rainy days to go crab hunting. There were plenty when it rained. We used bottle lanterns to see our way, along with a stick to hold them down when they crossed our path. When we caught them, we placed them in a big crocus bag. This is a sack, we used for carrying goods and produce to and from the market. This adventure was one of many which were led by my older cousin. After our catch we would come back and have a feast. I was what you would consider a tom boy. I loved to climb trees, but at the same time I loved playing in Aunt Pat's garden which had a stream of water running through it. She also had pigs and one of Deidre's and my chores were to collect scraps of discarded food from our neighbours to feed them.

Pee and Punishment

We had special nights that were set aside for slaughtering pigs. On slaughter night all the children had a can that was used as a pot to cook whatever part of the animal we planned to cook over the big fire. Those were fun times. There were nights all the children would gather around to hear Mr Casman's ghost stories. If you were smart you made sure you washed up before hand, as these stories would seem even scarier later in the night when you had to go to the toilet, which was located outside. I am not sure whether that was why I used to wet the bed or not. I used to have those dreams, that I was on the toilet peeing, but then I would wake up and realize that I never made it to the toilet.

Well, one night I had such a dream, and it so happened that Deirdre and I were sleeping in my aunt's bed. Aunt Pat woke us up, and asked which one of us had wet the bed. But of course both of us said we didn't, aware that saying you did would come with some sort of punishment. So what does my aunt do? She sent both of us outside to stay until one of us confessed. So there we were, the two of us, standing on our veranda out in the very dark night. It was pitch black out, and very scary. I am pretty sure Deirdre knew I was the one who had wet the bed, but being my big sister she didn't tell on me. After about half hour or so, my aunt had pity on us and called us back in. We still had to sleep on the wet sheets though, but at least we were inside. The next day, she made us take them out to hang out on the clothes line for all to see. I don't remember wetting the bed after that.

The Centre of the Commotion

One day while playing in a room that was unfinished (the flooring had not yet been completed) in Aunt Pat's house. I was jumping from the beams that were in place. I was having fun, jumping from beam to beam, and in my hand was the centre of an umbrella, the covering at the top part was broken. For some reason, I had one end of the umbrella in my mouth while jumping from beam to beam, when all of a sudden I missed the beam I was attempting to jump to and slipped. This brought the umbrella up into the roof of my mouth, almost at the back of my throat. I was bleeding profusely. I could feel a chunk of flesh hanging from the roof of my mouth and I remember thinking I was going to die. I cried out for help, and tried to explain what had happened. The one thing I didn't count on was that my aunt would be so upset for what I did, that she actually wanted to spank me right there and then. You see, Aunt Pat had just had eye surgery on one of her eyes, and wasn't in any mood to be dealing with a child who needed to be taken to the hospital from where she just came. I remember at this time we were standing outside and the neighbours had come out to see what all the commotion was about.

There I was, Aunt Pat holding on to one of my hands, and one of her eyes covered with bandages. The children in the neighbourhood were running around excitedly, the dogs were barking and then there were the neighbours who were begging my aunt to have mercy and not spank me. All I could think of was "Spank me already", so the drama that was happening around me would stop. Aunt Pat eventually took me to the hospital without spanking me. It was the first time I could remember going to a hospital. I hated it!

After being looked at by one of the doctors I was admitted. I was so afraid to be there, because I kept remembering a story I had heard about "crazy" patients who were located on the floor above me. They were known to come downstairs during the night hours to attack you while you were sleeping. To a little girl this was very scary. I ended up spending a few days in the hospital, but wasn't visited by any "crazy" person from the floor above. I was left with a large scar in the roof of my mouth as a reminder of that horrible day.

Usually when we had summer break from school my sister and I spent the time with my Grandma, my mother's mom. Going to my Grandma's house in the city for the summer was the highlight of my year. Grandma was very quiet but a strong woman, very independent. She was always humming one of her favourite church songs. She worked as domestic help for a rich white family. The husband was a doctor. Their house was big and beautiful. When we went along with my Grandma, we would have fun times playing in the back yard. It was a child's dream.

Grandma was a hard worker. She walked everywhere. There would be times that she would leave early in the morning, but before she left, Grandma had prepared our breakfast, which was always yummy. When she returned she came back with even yummier treats for us. One of my younger cousins was also living with my Grandma. She was our favourite cousin. She was a couple of years younger than Deirdre and I. We always had fun when we spent time with her. Grandma had a single house on a large piece of land that was fenced all around. She had flower beds and all sorts of large trees that bore such fruits as cherries, and mangoes, and even an almond tree.

One of my favourite things about being at Grandma's house was the fact that she had a television. This was at a time when most people didn't have one. There weren't a lot of channels, but the few channels we had gave us our first introduction to Sesame Street. We loved Sesame Street.

The few years I spent living in Jamaica were part of the most enjoyable times for me as a child. I loved the nature, the colourful water that surrounded me, and the games we children would invent when we came together, which was often. I loved the sense of community; someone was always looking out for you whether you were doing good or bad. But, the time came when all that would come to an end. My family was moving to Canada to join Momma.

Coming to Canada

I was ten years of age when my family moved to Ottawa, Canada. Just before we left, upon the insistence of Aunt Pat, I was baptized in her church, Deirdre too! She was only twelve. We along with our older brother left Jamaica with Daddy.

Living in Canada was a great joy in the early years; we were finally all together in one place. But it was so different being in a country where you no longer blended in, but stood out. We adjusted to the changes of our new world.

I liked my new school, but didn't like the fact that we dropped back a grade, because we were from another country. This change would affect me for the rest of my school days. It would make me the oldest child in my class, or cause me to be placed among the older children who had failed a grade, of which I wasn't one. We made friends at our new school. We learned to swim and skate. One of my earliest memories of Canada was the first time I met snow. We had heard the stories about it, and seen pictures. The day it arrived I was anxious to go outside to greet it. I was so anxious that I ran outside without any thing on my feet! Let's just say our introduction was very short, because as quickly as I ran outside, I was quickly running back inside for warmth. I chose to admire snow from the window inside my home. As the winter months came and went, I realized that snow wasn't always friendly or pretty.

April, one of my classmates, became my best friend. She lived with her Grandmother. They were from one of the other Caribbean islands. April's Grandma worked at the Governor General's house. I attended one of the garden parties given at the house once in the summer time; there were lots of people. The children took advantage of the lovely surroundings running and enjoying the grounds which were well groomed with beautiful flowers. It seemed as if there was an endless assortment of food constantly stacked on the tables. It was a great experience.

April and her Grandma were church attendees. Deirdre and I were invited to go along to visit one Sunday, and my parents agreed. My parents believed in God, but they were not churchgoers. Momma went ever so often, but most of the time, listening to Christian music or watching Christian programs on TV was what I remember of my parent's connection to Christianity. I enjoyed going to April's church. The people were friendly. We made friends there, so we kept visiting every chance we had. Unfortunately this didn't last very long. We moved to a different part of the city, so our visits to that church came to an end. We no longer attended that church, or any other church for that matter.

Loss of Innocence

Between the age of ten and eleven I was molested by someone that was dear to my family. This was a person whom my parents had entrusted to take care of me. The act of molestation left me confused in ways that would affect me for a very long time. There I was asleep in bed, when suddenly I felt the hands of a man lifting me up out of the bed I had occupied. It was early morning, because I could see the room as my eyes slowly opened unsure of what was going on. I was being transferred to another bed. I had no idea why until I felt my underwear being removed, followed by hands fondling me. Then I felt his genitals up against my private area where only I had had access to until this point. There was no screaming or words of objection coming out of my mouth. I laid there in silence, my mind racing trying to comprehend what was happening. I remember, while in the moment, thinking "This is wrong!" "I am just a child!" Even though it was taking place, it was as though it wasn't happening. I thought for a moment that maybe I had fallen asleep and I was dreaming, but of course this wasn't the case, because the physical and emotional feelings, along with the sexual sensation I felt stirring up inside me were very real. I never knew I could feel this way at such an early age.

As the years went by, I would remember this incident, but it was as if I wouldn't allow my memory to go beyond a certain point. I didn't know that the years ahead would be filled with such shame and guilt. And because of the guilt and shame that plagued me I would never speak about what took place that day to my parents or anyone. It would be a secret that I would bury deep within me for a very long time, until later on in my adult life this secret would resurface again and be released.

My first job came from a friend of my parents. Ms. Hillman worked as domestic help for a rich Canadian family. They lived in Rockcliffe Park, a place where a lot of people with money lived. She usually asked for my help mostly around the holidays, or when the people she worked for were going to have a party. I looked forward to having extra pocket money. We received money from our parents for the chores we did around the house, so this was an added bonus, as it meant more money to go shopping with! My job was to peel potatoes and carrots. They were very small, and there were a lot of them, but at twelve I was happy to be making money. I would sleep-over depending on how long it took me to complete the job. I didn't mind staying there; it was such a fancy house. Sometimes Ms. Hillman would have her own parties, and our entire family would be invited. Her parties were the best; lots of good food too! Everyone always had a fun time!

Momma also worked in the same area for an Egyptian diplomat as a server. Deirdre and I use to go with Momma to work sometimes. Their house was large, with a beautiful view of the water. We had a lot of fun playing outside. There were always tour buses passing by. The best part was when these tour buses came by, my sister and I use to wave at the people on the buses, and pretend we were living in that house.

Around that time Momma took Deirdre and I to a Government office to become Canadian Citizens. We were taken into one of the rooms as a family, where Momma had to do a test and afterwards place her hand on a Bible and take an oath. We were given small New Testament Bibles as gifts.

Our first house in Canada was an old duplex, which seem more like a pit stop. I was happy we didn't stay there too long. The best thing about that house was its location across the street from a school. After we moved there our parents brought us to Canadian Tire to get our first bikes, we were so excited that day. Neither of us knew how to ride as yet, so we had fun walking our bikes home, occasionally trying to have a ride. We used to have fun going to the school after hours learning how to ride our bikes. And because we were born in the same month we shared a birthday party there, which was a great teen birthday party. All of our friends were there. We had fun dancing and playing games.

My parents bought a new house shortly after that; it was so exciting moving into a new house. Our new house was located in a new area, just being built up. It was near a shopping centre; lots of kids lived in our neighbourhood. The most exciting part about our new house was that Deirdre and I each got our own rooms. Kendal had moved out and gotten his own apartment. Since moving to Canada we had to share a room, which was fun at times. I remember once we pretended to be singers, and movie stars. We turned the lamp over on the end table, which was between our twin beds and pointed it towards our big mirror, located in the centre of the room against the wall. It was like being in the spotlight.

Decorating our rooms the way we wanted was one of the best things. In our new rooms we each had our own TV and stereo with pictures of teen idols all over our walls. One of my favourite things to do was sing. I had a tape recorder that I received for one of my birthdays, and I would spend hours taping myself singing. My favourite song was "You light up my life" a song from the late 70's by Debby Boone.

In my early teens we started our new schools. I made friends, but was very insecure about my looks. I never thought I was pretty enough, plus I kept breaking out with blemishes all over my face. I did get very involved in sports at the encouragement of one of my teachers. I played basketball, volleyball, softball and ran track too. I was very good at sports, and enjoyed it.

As teenagers I remember Deirdre and I would beg Momma for us to get our ears pierced. Finally she took us to the shopping centre to get them done. We didn't mention it to Daddy, we knew he might object, we figured once its done there was nothing he could do about it. That was one of the happiest days.

In the middle of my teen years, you might say I blossomed. I was pretty good at doing my make-up, and styling my hair. I used to do other people's hair too, mostly braiding. When it came to putting my clothes together, I was good at this too! People use to always compliment me. That was always nice, but it was never a big deal to me. However, this skill would come in handy later on.

Violated Again

At the age of fourteen I was molested for the second time. I was sitting in our family's living room watching one of my favourite TV shows. I was disrupted by a knock at the front door. From where I was sitting I could peek around the corner and look down the hallway to see who was at the door. The main door was wide open, so I could see through the screen door. A friend of my parents who lived in the area was at the door. I gestured for him to come in and kept watching TV. Suddenly, I felt his hands on both my breasts, moving all over me; and a tongue in my mouth, like it was trying to locate something. I was in disbelief as to what was taking place, not only because I didn't expect this, but I thought how bold this man was to do such a thing as my dad sat in the basement of our home. I was so scared someone would approach us; what would they think? It seemed like a long time, but I know in reality it ended as quickly as it begun. The man proceeded to go downstairs to see my father. I was left in total shock, dismay, and so very violated. I never spoke to my parents about what happened, because this man was considered to be a close friend of our family. I knew if I was to mention this incident to my parents, it would cause a major fight. I didn't want to cause my parents any trouble. There was no doubt in my mind that my parents would have believed me.

After this incident, I steered clear, far away from this man; whenever I knew he was coming over I would go to my room and stay there. If we ended up being in the same room with each other we both pretended as if nothing ever happened. I hated the way he would look at me.

I became more aware of my changing body after this incident. I started to be more conscious of the way I dressed, the way I acted around any male figures. But I would still get the glaring eyes and even be propositioned by men who were old enough to be my father, or grandfather. I despised the way men use to "cat call" me on the streets. Especially the construction workers, I dreaded passing by them. All this would make me wonder what made these men act that way towards me. What was wrong with me? I felt like I was wearing a sign that said "Come and do whatever you want to Elaine, she doesn't mind!"

Later in my teenage years things changed. Things were not as much fun. I had been a very free-spirited child, the opposite of my quiet sister; this got me in a lot of trouble with Daddy, but even more so as I became a teenager. I always had a group of friends I would hang out with in high school. There were six girls in our group. There were a few extras that we just talked to, but the six of us were really tight. We had deep discussions especially about boys. We even formed a dance group and entered a dance contest at our school. We came in second place! We had so much fun when we would come together to practice. You could always find us hanging out in front of the school's gym. This is where all the cool black guys hung out. They were all into sports; the number one sport being basketball. We hung out with them, so I guess we were considered cool too. Some of the guys were seniors, so they were like older brothers; the older cooler girls were like our older sisters. We always had jokes when we all came together. Stories about something that happened to someone were always being told, or the teasing, but it was all in good fun. A few white kids were in the mix, but mostly if you would walk towards the gym, before school started, during lunch hour or briefly after school, you would always come across a large group of black kids hanging out there.

Daddy was a very giving man. I remember him coming home once with these make-up kits for us.

Another time he showed up with a Greek goddess statute. He had one for me and my sister, and a larger one for Momma. Until this day I still have my statue. It always reminds me of him. A favourite memory of my dad's giving nature was my sixteenth birthday. I was allowed to have a birthday party, and so I did. I invited my closest friends. Daddy had bought a case of beer for my party. I still remember the brand, Black Label. I know, some may frown upon this, but at that time, it meant the world to me. I felt Daddy understood how I felt somewhat. I had seen way worst things. I remember going to this girl's home and the parents would smoke up marijuana with them and their friends. Another girl I knew, seemed drunk all the time, and this was in grade eight. I remember once she had a party and there was so much booze. At my party, no one was drunk, or out of control, and my parents were home. Suffice it to say the party was a hit.

Restricted

Despite all of this, in my view Daddy was still too overprotective, and controlling. I was prohibited from going to movies or school dances or just hanging out with my friends the way I thought I should be allowed. I saw this as unfair and unreasonable. I felt restricted compared to my friends. So, I started to sneak out to attend parties, and have boyfriends, which wasn't allowed. Daddy would get very upset when he would find out. He was a man who believed in letting the belt speak for him. That's how he was raised, that's how he raised us. But when he did beat me, it didn't seem reasonable. It would cause an argument between him and Momma. Because of this my relationship with Daddy wasn't what I had hoped it to be. It was a relationship that made me a bit fearful at times and I distanced myself from him.

One particular incident happened at the age of sixteen. I wanted to go to a new place in town. By this time I was secretly dating a guy name, Rob. I met him through some friends from my neighbourhood. Actually, some people would say that it really wasn't dating; it wasn't dating in the normal traditional sense. You see we never went out on a date to the movies or spoke on the phone as normal teenagers did, and when we spent time together it was always in a group setting. On one rare occasion I received permission from Momma to attend a dance being held at one of the other high schools. This enabled us to spend some time hanging out together. Most of the time, we would see each other after school, where we would meet at the shopping centre close by my house. This particular shopping centre was where all the kids met after school. No matter what school you attended in the city, this was a central place where you could catch any bus to go directly to your destination or catch a connecting bus that did.

When we came together, there was a buzz about this new place among us. It was a place for young people and young adults to hang out. It was a place where you could roller skate indoors, and on the weekends it had an adjacent space that was used as a dance club. Every young person, that was into dancing and music wanted to go to this club. It was a place where all the cool and beautiful people hung out.

Of course Rob wanted us to go together. I really wanted to go, especially from all the fun I was hearing that you could have there. I asked Momma permission to go. She was lenient in such matters, more understanding and in tune with me as a teenager, than Daddy. I explained to her that I would like to go roller skating with some friends. Of course I left out the details of going with Rob, and also the part of my intentions to go to a club. By the time the weekend rolled around, I still had not gotten a yes or a no answer. So, I decided to get dressed and mention it again to Momma, hoping she would say yes. But there was a problem. Daddy was home. It was Saturday night. You see, usually during the week Daddy worked two jobs, one in the morning where he worked at a hospital, and another in the evening, as a cleaner in an office building. Daddy working in the evenings gave me a lot more freedom to hang out with my friends in the neighbourhood. Momma also worked at a hospital. Her shift covered part of the morning and part of the evening, giving me total freedom for about two hours. Momma would always make our supper in the mornings before leaving for work. Daddy would usually come home in between jobs to catch a nap or make our supper if Momma wasn't able to. With both my parents home I mentioned going out to meet some friends. This discussion didn't go too well. It ended with a no, and my response was that I was going to go any ways. Daddy said if I went, I couldn't come back home! At that moment all I was thinking about was the fact that I had already told Rob I would go, and had made plans to meet him at the shopping centre.

I left the house abruptly and started to walk towards the shopping centre to meet Rob. As I approached the bus stop he was waiting for me as we had planned. We waited for a bit until our bus arrived. Rob and I got on the bus with the other passengers, and sat down. We were having a conversation as the bus moved off, but then the bus stopped suddenly. I was looking in the direction of the driver as he was saying hello to someone, and to my surprise, Daddy came on the bus. I couldn't believe it! What was worse was the object my eyes were fixed on in his hand. It was a long tree branch.

There were no leaves on it. He was coming towards Rob and me, telling me to get off the bus. I didn't hesitate. I got up right away, afraid of what could happen if I didn't! I was too embarrassed to do anything else. I came off the bus through the back door. Daddy followed me all the way home walking behind me with the tree branch still in his hand. I entered our house and Momma was told what had just taken place. Momma said she never knew when Daddy left the house. A friend of the family was visiting, and he and Momma were trying to talk to Daddy about what he had done. "It was the wrong thing to do" they said. I went straight to my room feeling totally humiliated.

Suffice it to say that the relationship between Rob and I ended quickly after this incident. He moved on to date someone the total opposite of me. Someone he would be free to openly date, and go places with. From time to time I would run into them. It was never really friendly, as she always gave me dirty looks.

I met someone not too long after that relation-ship myself. I had stepped up my sneaking out of the house to attend house parties, which were plentiful. It seemed like there was one every weekend. It was at one of these house parties, I met Clay. He was into music, and would DJ house parties. Clay was a few years older than I was. He was working at a hospital and he had a car, which was very exciting. At times he would come and pick me up from school. I would skip classes to hang out with him, especially if it was towards the end of the day. Other times we hung out at his house, sometimes with his family. Clay lived with his dad, who was a single parent. He had an elder brother, and a sister that was a few years younger. His mom had left their dad some years before. I enjoyed my time with him and his family. They were fun to be around, and they were a close family. I was into him, so I did whatever it took to see him even if it meant sneaking out of my house to spend time with him.

Boiling Point

There comes a time when things have to change. Things came to a boiling point between Daddy and me. One day, I was at home by myself, sitting in the living room watching TV. Daddy came home, and the next thing I knew he was locking both the front door, and back door, which were usually left opened during the summer months. Without any explanation I saw him coming towards me. He was saying something under his breath, but from his tone, I knew it wasn't good. My eyes went straight towards the extension cord in his hand. It was positioned in his hand the way one of his belts would be before getting a beating. In the middle of all the thoughts that were racing through my mind, the one thing that held my attention wasn't that extension cord; but what I saw in his eyes. It was something I had never seen before. There was rage in my dad's eyes. Because of that look, I fought back, I fought hard. This didn't seem like my Daddy, the one I knew who loved me, cared for me, and worked so hard to give me the necessities of life. It was as though a stranger had entered our home and was attacking me. Somehow I ended up on the ground holding unto one of the legs of the sofa, kicking, screaming, and crying. Daddy stopped. I jumped up and rushed to my room, and stayed there until

Momma came home. Daddy beating me was one thing, but when it brought me to the place where I felt the need to physically defend myself, that was hard. We were never raised to disrespect or be physically abusive with anyone, especially not our parents. Momma was very upset that night because it seemed that Daddy always came after me when she wasn't home. I never knew what exactly triggered him to come at me with such rage. After that day, I realized the intensity of the problem between the two of us. I felt trapped and restricted, as though I was not living, as though I was being kept from what I thought was a normal life. Daddy saw my need to have some freedom as disrespectful, and disobedient. I decided that it was time for me to go. The home where I had many experiences, and memories, was no longer a happy one for me.

My best friend, Becky and I, often spoke about what was going on at home; she had a similar issue with her mom and step–dad. After filling her in on what transpired between Daddy and I, we made a plan to runaway from our homes together.

CHAPTER TWO

Runaway

O n a school day, Becky and I went to school as usual. We waited for the way to be clear to go back home to retrieve our belongings and leave for good.

When I arrived Grandma was home. She was living with us, as Momma had sent for her from Jamaica. I spoke to her briefly since I didn't want to give myself away. I grabbed some garbage bags discreetly, and went to my room and started packing the items I thought I would need the most.

According to our plan, Becky and I only had a certain time to collect our things. Becky lived around the corner and came to the back of our house to my bedroom window. She had already packed and had a taxi waiting. Quietly, I started to throw bags of my belongings through my bedroom window, as she would try to catch them, and bring them to the taxi. After I had thrown the last garbage bag out the window, I looked around thinking this is it! I'm leaving my home. I looked for Grandma, and said goodbye as if she would see me later.

I met Becky around the corner where she and the taxi were waiting. It was sad to be leaving, but at the same time I was excited for the independence and freedom that was awaiting me. Our planned destination was Becky's cousin's apartment. He was much older than us. His apartment was across the city from where we lived. Upon our arrival we paid the driver with money from our allowances.

We unloaded our belongings from the taxi and headed to the apartment where Becky's cousin was waiting to meet us. Becky introduced me to her cousin, but this introduction left me with an uneasy feeling. I didn't find him to be friendly towards me. I put my negative thought aside and figured maybe it was because we were about to invade his space.

I called Clay to let him know I had left home. He was surprised by this news, but understood. Speaking to him made me realize what a big decision I had made in leaving my home. I didn't think too much about what would happen. It wasn't something that I had planned or put a lot of thought into, but it was too late now. I also didn't think too much about how it would affect or impact the rest of my family, like Momma or Deirdre, until the next day when I was at school in class. My teacher instructed me to go to the office. When I got there I was told that my mom had called and wanted to speak to me. I took the phone and spoke to Momma, and of course she had many questions, which I tried to answer as best as I could in my reasoning for leaving our home. I felt sorry that I was putting Momma, through this. I heard her concern and felt her sadness, but I felt that I had done the right thing. I knew I couldn't allow myself to focus too much on how she felt. I gave her the number where she could reach me, and we ended the conversation.

News had spread quickly that we had left home. Cameo, a guy Becky had known through mutual friends, wanted to take us in and put us up in a motel and take us under his wings so to speak. The problem was that he and his business partners were known pimps around Ottawa. It wasn't something that was a secret or hidden. They would show up at parties all decked out with some girl on their arm, always looking the part. I wasn't about to go from leaving my home to be used by anyone for money or give them control over my life. I had to be in control now. I told Becky a definite no to any help from either of them. We had to support ourselves; we had to be working girls.

CHAPTER THREE

Working Girl

T he first thing we knew we had to do was to find jobs, but what kind of job? I was seventeen and Becky had just turned eighteen. We went through the want-ads and finally came across a job posting we thought we would be able to do. It was an ad for "Waitresses, Go Go Dancers." We weren't sure what it was about, so we called to enquire. When we called they asked us to come in to get more details.

The location of the place was in Hull, which was on the other side of the Ottawa River. It was an unattached building with a caricature of a nude girl on the outside. We went inside. It was very dark. It took us a few minutes to allow our eyes time to adjust to the darkness. We went down a flight of stairs and were met at the entrance by a guy, who seemed to be monitoring the door. We told him we were there to meet with the manager and gave his name. We were ushered into a large open space. It wasn't as dark anymore, because there were lights beaming from the bar against the wall, and from a large stage that was located in the centre of the room. It was occupied by a half naked girl dancing to extremely loud music.

We were standing by the bar for a bit, when a man came over to us, and introduced himself as Pierre the manager. Pierre was large in stature. He reminded me of a biker with his dark bearded face, along with his black t-shirt, black vest and jeans. We introduced ourselves and he took us aside to speak more in depth about the job description and its requirements. We were to take customers orders for their drinks, but were also expected to take turns dancing on stage.

Pierre called one of the dancers over to where we were; she was more mature looking than some of the girls I had seen passing by. He introduced us, and had her fill us in on what takes place while you were on your shift. This is how it worked. Each shift usually has about fifteen dancers, who take customer orders for their drinks, and take turns doing a set on stage. The set on stage required each dancer to dance to three songs. The first dance was supposed to be to a fast song, but there was no removal of your clothing, the second song could be a fast song or in-between fast and slow, which required you to dance while removing all items above the waist. Then the last song was to be a slow song, where you were required to remove the rest of what you were wearing, revealing all that you were given as a female. At the end of the song everything should be discarded.

We told Pierre we were not looking to take off our clothes, but were just looking to be waitresses. They both tried to convince us that it wasn't hard, and that there wasn't much to it. He said If we were not comfortable taking off all of our clothing, we could only remove the top part. Becky and I were looking at each other. We knew this wasn't what we had expected. We went back and forth trying to convince them that this wasn't for us; we finally agreed that we would try it as we were encouraged to do so. We watched a few girls to see what they did and how they went about doing it.

The Audition

The next thing I knew; Becky and I had picked songs we were familiar with. We were placed on staged at the same time because Pierre thought it would help with our shyness. The upbeat song of our choosing came on. We slowly took to the stage and started dancing the only way we knew how. It took a while during the second song for us to remove any clothing. We went through the motion, which seemed like having an out of body experience. The customers were encouraging and cheered. Not sure if it was because they saw how nervous and awkward we were, or if it was the fact that they were seeing two black girls on stage at the same time showing them all that we had. It was frightful, all those men watching us, some of the dancers too. I think what made it less scary was that I was with my best friend and we were going through this together. When the song finally finished, which seem like an eternity, we came off the stage, I felt relieved, excited that it was over, like it was a test and I passed. I couldn't believe we actually took our clothes off in front of a room full of strangers.

Becky and I were cute. I thought we were pretty and we had nice shapes. I was 5" and about 105 pounds and Becky was 5"1 about the same weight. I was more built in the chest than Becky, so months into dancing she would make the decision to get breast implants to make her breasts bigger. I tried to talk her out of it, but was unsuccessful. I didn't think they suited her body when she finally got them done; they were too large for her petite frame. I was happy with my breasts the way they were, plus the very thought of having something foreign in my body scared me.

As time went on I discovered a lot of the girls had implants, but you couldn't tell some girls had had surgery. It looked like they developed naturally that way, but there were other girls whose breasts were unnatural. You didn't have to look or think twice to wonder how "real" they were. They went way over-board in the sizes they chose for their body. A lot of girls had horror stories, and botched jobs, having to go from one doctor to the next trying to correct the work of the previous doctor, as much as they were able.

Sometime after her surgery, Becky started to have oozing of liquid mixed with blood coming out of one of her breast. I kept telling her to go see a doctor, but she kept putting it off. There was no urgency for her. I'm not sure what she ever did. We never spoke about it again.

After we finished dancing and got dressed, we were congratulated, and told how cute we were. This was a story that would follow us years later, whenever we would run into girls who were there that day when we first took to the stage.

We continued our conversation with Pierre. He gave us the information and the contact details of the agency located in Ottawa, where we could signed up. We thanked Pierre and left. We had a lot to say and think about on our way home, but came to the conclusion that we would go ahead and see where this would bring us as we felt there was no turning back now. The money that we could potentially make was more than anything we have ever earned before.

I still remember our first job together. We worked at a golf course trying to get people to buy raffle tickets for some promotion. We paid a percentage to the company we were working for. It was hard when people said "No", plus it was hot. The only good part about it was us hanging out together. My first real job after I received my social insurance number was working at a Revlon factory. I loved it as I was very much into make-up. I worked on the assembly line. As the eye shadow or blush would come off the conveyer belt, I would take the freshly made product and place them in a box. The best part of working there was the discount we had. They had an onsite room with lots of the Revlon products where you could purchase their products for a large discount, family included. After working at Revlon I got a position as a sales assistant, at a popular clothing store. I was asked to stand outside during sidewalk sales. It was a fun job. I enjoyed working outside in the summer, but it was hard on the feet. Becky and I also used to baby-sit, but none of those jobs would compare to what we were being offered.

Joining the Agency

The next day, we called the agency and made arrangements to stop by after school. It was an experience being there. We met with a man and sat with him in what felt like an interview. The office was in a stone building which was located on a street that I have been on many times. It is what you would probably imagine an agency representing strippers would look like. One thing I noticed was the many pictures all over the walls of nude girls, or partial nude girls. Some of the pictures were signed with messages on them.

We gave him all our information and in return got a run down on the workings of the agency. Basically, they would make the bookings for us, but mostly on the Quebec side initially, because we were still under age and would not be legal to work on the Ontario side. We would get our pay at the end of the week and he was sending us back to the club where we had auditioned. Our shifts would start at six in the evening and end at three in the morning, with an hour for supper. We also had a conversation about whether or not we would use our real names. This was something to think about. The agency was willing to book us right away. We were caught up to speed on what we would need. The agency also had outfits we could buy on display. We were allowed to get outfits, but it would be taken out of our pay, this seemed fair to us, so we tried on some outfits until we were satisfied.

There was a lot of lingerie one pieces, two pieces, different colours, styles and assortments. They were very pretty and very revealing, but I guessed that was the point. We got a couple of outfits for our new found profession. Later on, we learned that there were individuals who went around to the clubs selling outfits, but there was also one particular store in Hull where we could buy our dance wear. We ended our meeting and left the agency feeling good that we were going to start making money.

We spent time going through names that we thought would be good names for dancers. So,

Becky became Jessie and I changed my name to Chansie. Later, whenever I would tell customers my name, they would say "Take a chance on Chancy", I would respond by saying, "No that's not how my name is spelled". Sometimes it was a way to start a conversation with me. I would have this name for many years to come, even after I stopped dancing. So, with our new outfits, and new names, we became working girls.

One of the perks about joining this agency was being able to hire a driver. He would pick you up from your home if you had one, or motel room. He would drop you off at the club you were working. You could also request for him to pick you up after your shift. It cost a lot less than a taxi, and our rides were more personable, and at times you got the run down on what may have occurred at another club or with another dancer that day or night.

We learned early on that the agency didn't book you in a club if another black girl was already working there. So booking me and Jessie in the same club was just for a short period of time. Two black girls weren't booked on the same shift.

I guess it would be too overwhelming for the customers; too much Blackness. We would see each other in passing, and would pass on info as to the feel of the club for a girl of colour. The truth is, black girls were in demand, because first of all, there were only a few of us around, and second of all, we were stereotyped to be very sexual. With some men I discovered, it was their fantasy to sleep with a black girl. At times they made you feel like the forbidden fruit. It also worked in your favour, when it came to table dancing, especially if you had that one customer that could not get enough of you. It was fun when there were a larger number of girls in a club, because they would allow us to work together.

First Time Getting High

Another thing I became very aware of was the usage of drugs among the people in the clubs. Everyone seems to smoke cigarettes too. It was very rare to come across someone who didn't do drugs or smoke cigarettes. I had tried smoking cigarettes in my teen years, but I never liked the aftertaste or feeling as if I had bad breath all the time. It made me self-conscious; no matter how many times I would brush my teeth or how many breath mints I chewed on.

It was very common in the bars that when someone took out a cigarette that they would offer you one. The first time I did magic mushrooms or "shrooms" as they were called, I was working in a club over in Hull. A couple of the girls were about to do them, and asked if I would like to join them. I asked what they were and how they worked. They said I would have fun, and feel happy, and of course I wanted to feel good, plus I was still nervous taking my clothes off in front of all these people. I thought it would help put me at ease at the time. The mushrooms look like regular mushrooms, but dry. It tasted awful. I'm not a fan of regular mushrooms, so this didn't impress me at all. But I took them.

It felt like a few minutes had gone by, but I know it was longer than that. Eventually it was my turn to take the stage. I went up on stage and proceeded to dance, but everything seems to be moving in slow motion, I couldn't make out the music, it sounded slow and far away. I was losing touch with reality. Looking out on the customers, they seem to be laughing and talking about me, even the dancers seem to be talking about me. My heart was pounding, I felt anxious, I felt like I was standing in the middle of the room and had become the topic on everyone's lips. Later on when I looked back it reminded me of a movie I watched called, Carrie. I felt like Carrie, on stage, after the pigs blood had been dumped on her.

So there I was on stage having my Carrie moment. I walked off, I wasn't myself. The girls who I did the mushrooms with realized I wasn't handling this drug well. I kept saying, "Take me to Jessie". They asked me where she was working and I told them. I don't remember how I got to the club, but I wasn't fully dressed. I was so relieved when I saw Jessie; I tried to explain what had happened and what was going on with me. The next moment I was given milk to drink, lots of milk, and then I felt a cold compress on the back of my neck. I felt sick. I stayed with Jessie until the end of her shift. I eventually came down from my bad trip, of experimenting mushrooms. I found out later that magic mushrooms are a hallucinating drug, which can cause paranoia, loss of co-ordination, confusion, panic attacks and anxiety. After you have taken mushrooms, it really depends on your mood and your environment how the drug will affect you.

Many years later, I would try magic mushrooms again with my boyfriend at the time. It would be a very different experience. We were traveling on the Voyageur bus from Ottawa to Montreal where we were living. My boyfriend had gotten some mushrooms before he left, and wanted us to take them heading home. He was well aware of my not so good experience with it in the past. But since I felt safe and trusted him, I agreed to try them again. It wasn't too long into the trip after we took them, that things changed. The next thing I knew, it was as if we were waking up out of a deep sleep, I had no idea, what happened before that. We both started laughing for no real apparent reason. We were laughing just to laugh. Everything was funny. Our laughter grew louder and louder. I could not stop laughing. We laughed all the way to the end of our destination. Once we pulled up, we started to move to the front of the bus, because we were sitting in the very back. As we started to get off along with the other passengers it seemed some of the passengers had delayed their exit off the bus to see who these people were that were having such a fit of laughter, which made us laugh even more. Our laughter continued all the way home to our apartment. Everything we came in contact with was funny, even our cat being frisky. The experience was unlike the first in everyway.

The Ending of Things

Leaving home was the hardest decision I had to make, but I found myself making harder decisions as I went along. One of the decisions I had to make came weeks after Jessie and I left home. We had been working at the clubs in Hull and Gatineau which closed at 3:00 am; they were unlike the clubs in Ottawa, which closed at 1:00 am. We were still trying to go to school and work at the same time, but the hours we worked were making it very difficult to get up and get to school on time. After a while we were just showing up whenever.

During this time I got out of touch with school. I lost the schedule for my classes, and became confused, as to which class I should go to and at what time; I had no idea where I was suppose to be. I would spend most of my time in the cafeteria or the girl's bathroom. I wasn't about to speak to any of my teachers about my new living arrangements or situation. While this was going on with me, Jessie had already stopped going. As we were not working in the same club, we would see each other during the days. Eventually, I was so tired physically of going to school, and feeling like I was wasting my time, I stopped going. Who would have thought I would have quit going to school in the tenth grade? Not long after I left, we found out that a rumour was going around our high school that we had become strippers.

My relationship with Clay ended dramatically. He hated the fact that I was working as a stripper. It was hard for him to accept me doing such a job. The break up left me heartbroken. It affected me in a big way. I really enjoyed having him in my life, but on the other hand I thought it was the only thing I could do that would help me to stay free and have my independence, while making enough money to survive. Being in the situation I was in, with no place to stay, I felt I had to stay with the job that was giving me money, at least for that period of time. I didn't see any other option.

Jessie and I decided to work out of town. We felt the chance of running into someone we knew was less likely. And since I was feeling down about my break up with Clay, I was up for anything that would distract me, or take my mind off him. The best thing about working out of town was our salary; because you made more money when you were booked out of town. We also found out from some of the other dancers that it would be best to go through an agency in Montreal in order to get bookings there and in the surrounding towns. They could always book us back in Ottawa if we wanted. So that's what we did. We got in touch with an agency in Montreal, and of course they wanted to see us in person.

The first thing we did upon our arrival in Montreal was to leave our bags in a locker at the bus depot, and then head for the agency. We found the agency, and at first glance it seemed a bit fancier than the one in Ottawa. After going through all the details and information needed, we were told to check back with them the next day, as they had no way of contacting us. We had decided previously that the best place to stay would be at the YWCA. The daily rate was low, but we also had a curfew, so we had to be back by 11:00 pm, and this was very new to us.

Going to the Y was not a good experience. I didn't like the feel of it, or the look for that matter. You had to share the bathroom, and kitchen area, but thankfully we wouldn't have to stay there too long, or so I thought.

The next day, after a not so restful night, we left to check out the stores around us. We didn't have much money, so we were trying to spend it wisely. We wanted to stay close to the Y, as not to miss our curfew, so we decided to go and check out the club where most of the male dancers from Montreal who would visit Ottawa worked. We were actually looking for two male dancers in particular, Rico and Toni. They were male dancers we had met upstairs from the bar we had first started working. Toni was very handsome; he was tanned with piercing blue eyes, and an excellent dancer. He was French, extremely friendly, and popular with the ladies. He knew how to work the room. He was what we would consider a professional. Jessie really liked Toni, to the point where she would even get him to table dance for her, which I thought was funny, a dancer paying another dancer to dance. Jessie was so infatuated with Toni she thought it would be a great idea if I hooked up with his friend Rico. Rico was the darker version of Toni; more reserved, and to the point. I didn't find him to be as friendly; but he was also an excellent dancer. We never hooked up, he wasn't my type and I don't think I was his either, but we were friendly with each other.

Our trip to the club to look for Toni or Rico was a waste of time. We asked about them, but were told they were not working there that week. So, we ordered ourselves drinks, spent a bit of time checking out the other dancers, grading them, and then we left.

We checked with the agency the next day, but no booking as yet. This went on for some time. While waiting we were running out of money. We thought we would have been working by now. We had spent most of our money on helping with rent at Jessie's cousin and of course shopping.

During the day we would leave the Y and walk the streets, making it back for our curfew at night. We wanted to make sure we had somewhere to sleep, so we didn't spend much of our money on food, so by now we were getting really hungry. I remember being so hungry at one point that I was hoping someone would discard some food item in the garbage can, so I could have something to eat. I didn't care at that point because I was so hungry.

We were tired of walking up and down the streets of Montreal. Thank God it was summer time. About the fourth day we decided to go into a restaurant to use the washroom and freshen up and maybe get some fries out of the little bit of money we had left between the two of us. We had no idea what we were about to encounter. As we walked into the restaurant an older lady started coming towards us yelling, waving her arms around, speaking in French. I had no idea what was going on, but Jessie, who did speak French knew what she was saying. She wanted us out of the restaurant; because she thought we were prostitutes! I was so shocked and embarrassed, because there were quite a few people in there. It was the worst feeling to know that she thought that we were coming into her establishment to solicit her customers.

We quickly walked out humiliated. But it didn't end there, while we were trying to kill time walking up and down popular St. Catherine Street, we stopped at a certain corner not sure what to do with ourselves, we were approached by some girls who were dressed like prostitutes. They made it known what they were. They also made it known that we were infringing on their territory. We apologized, trying to get them to understand that we weren't working girls, but they didn't care to hear what we had to say. Once again we quickly left the scene.

Years later, whenever I would mention this encounter to someone in my life, the question was always, "How were you dressed?" I am not sure how we were dressed exactly, except to say we usually dressed in what we thought dancers wore. We thought we were fashionable. Jessie and I had gone shopping over in Hull with our first pay, and I guess our attire was appropriate for our new profession. Looking back I guess we did dress in a way that most would consider sexy, but not with the intention of picking anyone up. We were supposed to dress sexy when we went to the agency. We saw the way the other girls looked when they came from Montreal and we wanted to look just as good, or better. We always wore heels, or fitted outfits that of course showed our curves. We also had purchased these boots, they were cream, with heels, and went all the way up to our thighs. I loved those boots! I would dance in them later, a lot. I usually didn't feel completely naked when I wore them.

The Proposition

It was getting late in the evening, so we decided to go to a nearby park to hang out. We were approached by a couple of men, and they started up a conversation with us. Small talk really, but the conversation eventually went to an invitation of going back to one of the guys place to hang out. They said they would pay us to spend time with them. We didn't even really think about it, we were so tired, and hungry. To go to another place besides the Y, which wasn't all that appealing in anyway, therefore this invite sounded really good to us at the time.

We drove back to one guy's place. It was "homey" not bad for a guy's pad. We got something to eat, and of course, the men were having some drinks. Before I knew it Jessie was off with one of the guys. I was left with the other. I felt uncomfortable, and I wasn't sure what to say. We started with small talk again. He mentioned taking a shower and sug- gested that I join him. All I was thinking about was getting the money and getting out of there. With that thought in mind I agreed. I went off to the shower with him. Being in the shower with that man was one of those moments where I wished I could have snapped my fingers and disappeared. The only thing I could allow myself to think about was that I needed his money. We ended up staying the night as we had missed our curfew to go back to the Y.

There I was sleeping in one of the rooms, when the guy I was with came in and decided that he wanted more than to take a shower with me. I said no to have sex with him, but he became forceful, like whatever I said, he couldn't hear or understand. I kept pushing him off me, and calling out for Jessie. But there was no Jessie to come to my rescue. I kept trying to fight him off until finally he got mad and gave up exiting the room. Morning could not come soon enough for me. I was really upset with Jessie for not coming to my rescue. Her response was that she thought I was just fooling around. Jessie was given two hundred dollars from the guy she was with. We took a taxi back to the Y. We had officially prostituted ourselves for money.

The next day, we went to another male strip club and met a guy who was a photographer. He took pictures of strippers. He asked us if he could take some pictures of us, and since we didn't have much to do while we waited for a booking with the agency, we agreed. We agreed to meet him at his place. We were just happy to be visiting and hanging out with someone other than ourselves, and not for sex. It was a nice old house that was partly a home, but also seemed to double as a studio. He gave us the run down on some of the pictures around his house and then got right to work taking pictures, as it was all about the lighting. He took pictures of me and Jessie individually, and then some with each other. He was very much into taking pictures of us partially nude, or nude; it was "art", as he would say, so we allowed him. We felt comfortable with him, and we were actually having fun. It was a change to be having fun with all the negative experiences we had had so far. He made us a nice dinner and introduced us to his roommate when she got home. She worked in a club as a waitress. We stayed all day, and then headed back to the Y for the night. We never did go back for our pictures because the next day we called the agency and were relieved to know we had both been booked in a few clubs. Looking back at that time, I realize somewhere out there; there are nude pictures of me. At times I wonder whatever became of them.

We began working in small town clubs in the surrounding area of Montreal. Some of these towns I had never heard of before. I hated some of them because they were old and rundown.

There was one place I stayed at that reminded me of a horror movie. It felt eerie; all these flies kept showing up in my room. I had no idea how they were getting in. That hotel reminded me specifically of The Shinning with Jack Nicholson for some reason. I never watched the movie in its entirety because I don't like scary movies all that much, but I remember scenes from it. This hotel was right out of that movie.

At these clubs I was considered the feature dancer for the week. I met some nice people and some not so nice people. One night I met a guy who was at one of the clubs I was working at. He and his rock & roll band were also staying at the hotel. He was the drummer. They would be playing there for the weekend. He invited me to come and check them out, so later that evening I decided to go, since I had nothing else to do in my free time in such a small town. I had no one to talk to or hang out with, as Jessie was booked at other clubs. So, it was either I went or stay in my room, which usually I did when I was working in the towns, because I wasn't interested to venture out to do anything.

I went to see what they were all about and was pleasantly surprised. They were actually good. The drummer and I talked in between sets, and after they were finished playing for the night he asked me if I wanted to do a hit of acid. He showed me a square white paper blotter. It was the tiniest thing. I had never taken acid before, so I asked him what it would do to me. He said I would feel happy, and of course since I hadn't been feeling all that happy, it sounded like the thing for me. He explained that you put the paper under your tongue and so I did, and it dissolved. The next thing I knew, the music sounded loud. One moment it was loud the next moment it sounded far away. Everything became very colourful around me. The people looked out of the ordinary with funny faces, but I felt good, light. My new friend and I hung out, we had a few drinks. I was feeling happy. It was fun, to be with someone. I was laughing so much, seemed like everything was funny. We ended up going back to his hotel room and I spent the night with him. He gave me his home number where I could reach him. He lived close to Toronto. I said I would call, which I did when I returned to Ottawa. I spoke to him, and we had a good conversation, but I never called again. I wasn't interested in a long term or long distance relationship at the time.

Finally, it was the end of the week. I was heading back to Ottawa after weeks of going from town to town, club to club. I had had enough, I had been so lonely, working in the clubs by myself, it seemed that's all these towns could afford was one girl for the night crowd. These places were without a DJ. It was me and a juke box and I would get the money from the bartender. I was very anxious to go back to what was familiar, what I considered civilization.

I went back to Jessie's cousin's place, but things felt very uneasy, not to mention that I found out that Jessie and her cousin had been intimate with each other. She tried to explain that they weren't really cousins by blood. They were related through her step-father, and that it didn't count. With this new information I felt even more uncomfortable. I wanted to leave, but wasn't sure where to go. After a lot of thinking I came to the conclusion that the best thing for me to do was leave.

A few days went by, and I felt more out of place than ever before, so I called the agency I was with in Ottawa. They were able to get me a booking to work and also a motel room. I packed my things and headed to the motel, very happy and relieved to be leaving.

Motel Living

The motel set up was interesting. There was a section of motel rooms allotted to the agency, which was located close to all the clubs in Hull. Whether it was just a regular dance club or a strip club, it was conveniently close to restaurants for eat or order in. Sometimes, you could end up sharing your room with another dancer or you could end up having the room all to yourself, which I liked better. Only if you were booked that week, could you have a room or if you were working from one week into another week steady. As long as you were booked you could stay in the room. If there was a break in between your booking you had to pay for your room or find somewhere else to stay until you were booked again.

I began working steadily in the clubs. One of the regular happenings of working in the clubs was these unannounced visits of the police officers. They would come around to check the girls ID's to make sure that we were of age to be working in the clubs. This was a problem for me, because I was still under age. Whenever they would show up, I would have to go in the back and hide until one of the girls would let me know when they had left.

This wasn't the only time I ended up hiding from someone who came in the clubs. I remember working at one of the clubs in Ottawa and two of my teachers from high school walked in. One of them was my English teacher. Thank God I saw them before they saw me. I rushed to the back where we had our changing room. I let one of the girls know what was going on. She in turn passed it on to the other dancers and the DJ, so he wouldn't start playing my song and expect me to show up on stage. Usually, unless you went to change your songs for your set, you would hear the DJ announce your name to be next, and then you would hear your first song start playing, which was your cue to take to the stage. No matter what you were doing or where you were coming from you had to leave it and take the stage.

Sometimes you could be table dancing and you would have to hurry to get dressed just to take your clothes off all over again. The preference of course, was to have time to freshen up before your set, or to perhaps change your outfit. As I went along I learned how to time myself before my set, and kept track of the list that was used by the DJ to mark the order of each dancer. Usually, you were placed in the order of which you went to see the DJ to pick out your songs for your set.

In Hiding

So, there I was hiding. I was in hiding for a while. One of the girls would come back regularly and update me about what was taking place. The waitresses had tried to hurry them along. As soon as they finished their drinks the waitress would remove the empty bottles or glasses, but then they would just place another order. Trying to get them to leave went on for some time until finally they left. Strangely enough I wasn't as surprised to see my English teacher there, as I probably should have been. I remembered back in high school, how he would look at one of my friends. She was cute and had large breasts; I would catch him glaring at her constantly. After his first appearance in the club I would see him again from time to time over the years, but since my name, and looks had changed I knew he didn't recognize me and after awhile I didn't care anymore.

These occasions where I would run into familiar faces occurred every so often. At one club where I was working I saw one of my dad's closest friends. I made sure to avoid him. The DJ's were always understanding about what was going on, so they never forced you to go up and do your set. On another occasion, some of the guys from my high school who I used to hang out in front of the gym with showed up. But after awhile I just got used to seeing people I knew.

Experiencing Racism

I can remember my first real experience of racism in the clubs while dancing at one of the clubs. I was booked at a club in Carlsbad Springs, just outside of Ottawa boundary. I was happy to be working with a dancer who was at the club when Jessie and I first took to the stage. She was young, but was motherly, she was very helpful in giving me the run down on what to do and what not to do in the business. She reminded me of a biker chick, because she wore a lot of black and leather.

There was a few of us girls booked at the club that week. I was on stage doing my set when I heard some ruckus coming from some of the girls. The next thing I knew the dancer who had been motherly towards me was in a fight with one of the other girls. There I was on stage watching the fight unfolding before me. I stopped dancing. The manager and the bartender broke up the fight. After the dust had settled, my friend had gotten stabbed in one of her legs. Thankfully it wasn't too bad. The girl that had stabbed her turned out to be part of the Hell Angel's Biker gang. The manager fired both of them for fighting. Because of this incident, another dancer and I decided to leave with our friend. We got dressed and called for a driver to pick us up. My friend told me what caused the fight. Apparently the confrontation came about because the Hell Angel's dancer made a racist comment about having to work with a black girl. My friend wasn't impressed with her attitude and told her, which is what lead to an argument, which lead to the fight.

I felt really bad that my friend had gotten stabbed, but was thankful that she stood up for me. We got dropped off at my friend's place and called the agency to inform them of what happened. We were able to get another booking, but not together. At least we were booked elsewhere and we didn't lose a week's salary. I think because of the circumstances the agency was considerate and booked us somewhere right away. Usually, if you wanted to be booked in one of the better clubs for the following week, it was best to call before the end of the week. I had never experienced any other obvious racism while dancing after this incident. If there were those who didn't care for my presence they kept it to themselves. They wouldn't say so verbally, but I could always tell by their body language.

Christmas Alone

My first Christmas after leaving home, was one of the worst Christmases ever. I was working at a popular club, during the Christmas season, and the club was closing down. I learned that men don't come to strip clubs during the holidays, because most of them were married, family men, and those who weren't married still had somewhere else they needed to be. One of the club's bouncer and I became very friendly. He was a former boxer, and apparently famous. I didn't know who he was, but I saw the pictures from his fighting days. He was good looking, and a charmer. He said he would come by my motel room to spend some time with me, so after the club closed, he came to my room. He was there for a bit and eventually we started kissing and one thing lead to another. Not too long afterward he said he had to go to a family get together. I was very disappointed. I was under the impression that he would be spending the evening.

So, there I was all by myself with no one to spend Christmas with. It never even occurred to me to go home for Christmas, or even call. I later found out that he was involved in a serious relationship with someone. They were engaged. I didn't think it was a very serious relationship if he was still sleeping around. I felt so used and hurt. I was just a one night stand. I couldn't even say one night because he only spent a few hours with me, then he was gone.

When I ran into him again, I let him know that I was aware that he was in a relationship, and there was no way he was coming near me again. After this experience, I realized that he wasn't the only one who slept around or had someone on the side. This type of behaviour seemed to go hand in hand with the club life.

Stolen ID

One night, after working my shift I discovered that someone had stolen my hand bag. There was no money in it. I learned early on to carry all my cash on me. When I had to do my set, my money went into one of my shoes. They took the whole purse, which held my ID's: my passport, Canadian citizen card, and birth certificate. I had taken all my documents, except my Jamaican passport with me when I left home.

Whoever took my ID had no idea the problems they would create for me later on. All through my years of working in the clubs I had no ID. When I tried to get copies of my documents I had nothing to prove my actual date of birth. Later, when I tried to get another copy of my birth certificate, I discovered there had been a fire and I was only able to get my registration form. The thing about that is it had the date that I was registered, as my date of birth. My Jamaican passport also had the wrong date. Eventually, after many years and many tears, I had to use the date that I was registered as my date of birth. I always had to remember to give the registration date rather than my actual date of birth, whenever proof was required. I had blamed my parents for not making sure all my documents were in order and correct. I felt as though no one was paying attention, otherwise all the mistakes would have been corrected long ago, or never taken place at all. But in the end I had to take responsibility for not protecting such important documents, for being careless, and I guess a bit naïve.

It was a wakeup call for me. It made me realize the type of people that I was surrounded by. As time went on I came across liars, crooks, people who seemed to create their own world based on lies. And the worst part of it was that they believed their lies. I was finding it harder and harder to believe anything that came out of anyone's mouth. I was becoming sceptical of everyone. It was all about getting what's theirs, or what they thought was theirs. It was all about pleasing themselves first, and forgetting everyone else. My perception of people was changing. I knew I wasn't cut out for the club life.

CHAPTER FOUR

The Club Life

With my new identity in the club life I was now in full swing. I was very surprised that I was in such a profession, as I didn't think of myself as very pretty or shapely. From my teens I struggled with self-confidence, and self-esteem. But here I was, not sure why I would put myself in the position to be judged.

Working in the different clubs allowed me to come across and work with all types of girls. There were girls who were the real educated student types, dancing to put themselves through college or university. They attended classes by day, danced at nights. Then you had the single moms, who left their kids with someone in the family or a babysitter. There were those who had kids and lived common-law with the father of the kids or their boyfriends, and worked to make ends meet. Then you had the runaways like me.

Dancers Not Strippers

We were mostly referred to as dancers, which I didn't mind as much. I preferred that rather than being referred to as a stripper, which sounded insulting. It seemed harsh and degrading. Maybe it was because when I heard the word "stripper" it was often used in a negative way. I met some girls who were actually excellent dancers, who could do a lot with their bodies, and some you could tell had a background in ballet dancing. Then there were those who I considered to be real striptease acts, in the true sense of the word, like what I remember from those old movies. I considered myself a dancer.

As I was going along, I was learning a lot from other girls and was becoming more and more in-tune with my body. I was learning how I could manipulate it in a lot of different ways. I never knew I could move my body that way.

For me it was all about the dancing, it was my focus. I usually expressed myself in dance according to the words of the songs. Some days, I really didn't pay too much attention to the customers, I just danced. It felt good when I was complimented for my dancing. After my set, I always felt as though I had been to the gym for an intense workout. I was actually becoming a very good dancer.

The waitresses we worked with were very nice. They always had our backs as dancers, unless you just weren't a nice person, which was the case for some of the dancers. Some of the waitresses were ex-dancers, and looked like they could take the stage anytime. They made good money, and were frequently tipped well. Most of the waitresses were good at their jobs. They juggled all those drinks on one tray, or in their hands, and remembered their orders, while still handling those customers who pestered them to take the stage. Secretly, I envied them. I just wanted to serve drinks, which I was getting the hang of, rather than having to choose a set of songs, go up on stage, and take off my clothes in front of a bunch of men, hoping that they would like me enough to cheer while I did my set.

Most customers wanted to buy you a drink. It went with the atmosphere. We girls would be sitting at our table (there was always a table for the dancers of the clubs.) A customer would come over to speak to you directly, or a waitress would approach you on their behalf wanting to know what you were drinking. In the beginning, I wouldn't take a drink or if I did I gave it to one of the other dancers without the customer knowing. Customarily you would get your drink and then join that customer. This would lead to conversation and table dancing.

Table Dancing

Table dancing was the big thing. To provide a customer with a table dance you used a stool made out of wood. That was round in diameter on top, with a base in the middle. There was just enough space to hold one person. It was only a couple of feet off the ground. You would carry it over to the customer's table, or if the customer was nice enough they brought it to the table for you. Sometimes if it was a large group, they had more than one dancer at the table. The goal was always to have a customer ask you for a table dance after your set. Sometimes all it took was for a customer to ask you to dance, and then you became popular for the night. Men can be very competitive; therefore it could work in your favour. I hated table dancing. Inside I would be upset when someone asked me, because it meant being up close and personal. I would sit and hope no one would ask me, but it made a difference how your night ended financially. There were times that you could end up spending a whole shift with one customer because he was willing to spend money on you for a night of table dancing. In between dances you would go else-where, but return later at the request of the customer. I didn't mind doing this because it made my shift go by faster. If it was someone you were having a good time with, it was all the better for you.

The worst was when there were a group of guys drinking. It could be a stag night for someone getting married, a party for someone retiring, or someone's birthday. Some groups were fun. But some would get out of control, or too rowdy when the men would try to touch you, which was a no-no. That would lead to a confrontation with the customer and could end with someone, or the whole group, being thrown out by the bouncer. I hated the fights. They always made me sad to see how one moment people were celebrating having a wonderful time and the next moment they were bloody. It was worse when you liked the group. It could be one person out of control having had too much liquor, and then the whole group had to go.

The goal was always to have that one customer who didn't mind spending his money to satisfy his need and in the process make you happy, like a sugar daddy. He would send you flowers, show up with gifts to surprise you, and to tell you the truth it was a good feeling. There were some customers who followed you from club to club.

Table dancing was such a game. You would show a little bit more for more of that "cash." Having that one customer who was guaranteed to be at one particular club was comforting in that you knew someone would be there to make some cash off.

But that one customer can be scary, creepy, when you would stop and think about it. I remember having this one particular customer that became a regular of mine. While dancing for him I mentioned making money for a bill that was overdue. It was a large sum of money. It was surprising to me when he offered to help me pay my bill. Of course I declined, but he insisted so I finally agreed. He brought the funds the next day!

I suggested we meet at a plaza close to my house. What happened next scared me. Before I could get to the plaza, which was in walking distance from my house, I saw the white van he had told me to look out for. I was shocked to see it approaching me. I felt uneasy, and it took me off guard. A lot of things were racing through my mind, and I started to wonder if he had seen which house I came out of, or whether he had followed me home. I was worried that he might know where I lived.

He stopped close by me, and we said hello to each other. He said he went to the plaza, but thought that since he hadn't seen me he would drive around to see if he would meet me on my way. I learned a major lesson that day. I realized the danger I was inviting into my life on so many levels by this customer knowing the neighbourhood in which I lived. Seeing a customer from a club, especially during the day in a different environment, was a totally different experience. It was something I would never do again.

The Unconventional

Very strange and kinky people came through the doors of the clubs. There were those customers who had different fetishes, like the customer who had a thing for boots. Wearing my thigh high cream boots was a complete turn on for him. Then there was my encounter with a married couple. During one of my shifts, a waitress approached me to tell me that there was a request for a husband and wife to see me. I went over, and they asked me to dance for them. I was completely taken off guard, and had not expected such a request. But I pretended it had not affected me. This was a new and strange thing for me. I went through the motions dancing for them with my focus on the husband. It just felt unnatural dancing for a man, with his wife sitting right there, watching me, expecting me to include her as part of the package. I did it, and when it was all over, an even stranger request came; it was for me to accompany them to their home.

This was even more bizarre to me. Of course I declined. I learned from some of the girls who had come across them before, that they were considered to be "swingers", which meant they had no problem sharing each other sexually with outsiders. Some of the girls were used to dealing with such couples in this area, but it made me think about the sanity of people. Why even bother getting married if you still desired to be with someone else? I guess that wasn't the point.

Working with Male Dancers

The club where we had auditioned the first time became one of the clubs I worked at in the beginning. It was popular, always busy; you could make lots of money on your shifts. This club had another club upstairs, it was for the ladies, and it was the place to go to see male dancers. Upstairs was the reverse of what was going on downstairs. At times I would work upstairs with the male dancers, along with other girls; it was more to appease the few males who would accompany their ladies. The club was very busy on weekends, especially for bridal showers, and birthdays. We considered the female customers worse than the men in some ways, but in other ways they were the same. Have you ever seen a scene in a movie that shows a bridal party, or girlfriends hanging out at a male strip club? Then you see them get very loud, screaming at the dancers to "Take it off!" It's actually depicted correctly. At times I felt sorry for the male dancers, the women were not merciful. They were very bold, and some were quite rude, from a woman's point of view. They would try to place money in the male dancers G-strings. Sometimes there were those females who would get so drunk they would try to kiss the dancers. They would get very touchy with their hands all over them. The male dancers would always try and laugh it off, because of course, if you wanted to make money you had to put up with some degree of vulgar remarks, just like the female dancers. I found the bouncers at the door to be more lenient on the women than they would ever be with the men. As a female dancer you hated to be sent upstairs, but I did my time and happily returned downstairs.

Some of the male dancers were really nice. Others thought they were God's gift to the female population. Some were even in serious relation-ships. Years later I would come across dancers who were dating other dancers. I guess like any job you can relate better to someone who was in the same profession.

While working upstairs I came across a guy I thought was interesting. I found out quickly about his obsession with playing a video game called, Centipede. He drove a bright yellow Firebird. I liked his car. I was into Trans-Am's and Firebird's at the time. His car was pretty to look at, with the bird all laid out on the hood. Years later I would buy a Trans Am, but would never end up driving it. This guy was very good looking, but his focus was always on sucking back his beer, playing his favourite game and trying to beat the highest score, which of course, was his. A few of us would gather around to watch him play. I found him fascinating because he never really paid much attention to the goings on in the club except for a few comments here and there. We would have short conversations, but then he was gone.

The video games in the clubs came in handy for those quiet times. You could spend a large sum of money sitting there. Some of my favourite games to play were Pac Man, Ms Pac Man, or playing the Pinball machines. I spent hours playing these games. A club with a pool table was fun too. Some clubs had rules about how you had to be dressed around the pool table; you had to be covered up.

There were also clubs that showed pornographic movies. There was one particular club that I would work at in Aylmer, mostly on Sundays. This club showed porno films all the time. I considered them degrading, obscene and vulgar. No one should be exposed to such things. The story lines were so tasteless, senseless, and meaningless, along with the loud moaning and groaning. They always irritated me. I could never bring myself to watch them.

I was happy that it was only a few of the clubs that played them. Most clubs had the TV's set on the sports channel.

Special Feature

At times, I would end up working at a club that had a special event with a featured dancer. I remember a dancer who I would consider a professional because she had been in the business for some time. She would be paid big money to come to that club. They, in return, would make big money on all the attendance charged at the door, along with the alcohol they would sell while she was there. This dancer in particular danced with a tiger. It reminded me of something you would see at a circus. It was very dramatic-fire and all! I tried to stay clear of that tiger when they brought it out of its cage for her to do her show. I wasn't going to trust my life around such a large animal no matter how beautiful it was to look at.

During my time of going from club to club I ran into Jessie. After what happened at her "cousin's" place I just went it alone. She mentioned she had left his apartment right after I left. We hung out sometimes and even ended up sharing the same motel room. I didn't always like sharing rooms with her because she was very messy. But, we did have fun hanging out together and having conversations about the customers we came across.

One day we both had the day off, and spent the day hanging out in our room. We decided to make a list of all the guys we had slept with along the way. Well, let's just say our lists were very long. It's a good thing that one of the first things we did when we left home was to go to a community health centre to put ourselves on birth control. I was surprised at my list, because a lot of times I was very picky as to whom I would even have a conversation with. Considering the amount of men I came across on a weekly basis I didn't consider my list to be so bad.

Other Options

There were ways you could make extra money as a dancer. One way was to do private stag parties at a hotel or in someone's home. You could go with another dancer, or sometimes there would be more girls, depending on how large the group was. A bouncer would go along to make sure we were safe. A set payment was paid up front upon our arrival, which would be divided amongst the dancers, and the bouncer. Our time would be spent dancing and mingling with the group, which was about an hour. This wasn't an option that I was comfortable with. The group usually got rowdy. I preferred to freelance.

Freelancing came in handy when you worked the day shift and you didn't make enough money, so you would go to another club to ask if you could work. They didn't mind, because it was an extra girl that they didn't need to pay any salary to.

Some girls would suddenly show up to free-lance. I did this too, but some girls would come just to hang out rather than take the stage. There were girls who had never danced before, but after a few drinks, were drunk enough and wanted to try it. In other clubs this was unacceptable. Some clubs allowed freelancing, only if they didn't have too many girls already scheduled.

Having a freelancer was good because it gave you a break. The more girls, the fewer sets you had to do, which I was always happy about. It gave me more opportunities to table dance if needed. At the same time, there were those newer customers who came in, and usually wanted to see you do your set before asking for a table dance. If the girl free-lancing started to become popular for table dancing, because she was new on the scene, it could cause a bit of a riff with those who were scheduled to be there. Some girls would freelance if they took time off from working a regular shift. They would come in, make their money, and leave. If they were not making any money they moved on to another club.

Good Show

It was during our time of freelancing, that Jessie and I started to do duos together. This was after a few drinks of course. If I went to visit Jessie at the club she was working at, or visa versa, and we wanted to spice things up, we would do a duo. This wasn't an unusual event.

We moved the same way and it made for a good show. We had a way of moving our bodies like what people would say was like a "snake." We twisted and slid our waist a lot when we danced. We both wore a belt that would wrap around our waists, which I believe help make our waists seem really small. Jessie was a very good dancer. She knew how to do the splits and was toned too, but my body was thicker. My muscles seem to pop out more than hers.

The men always liked it when two girls did a show together. Jessie and I would join each other while about to do the last song, which was called your floorshow. It was very erotic, intimate. Moving as close to each other as possible was the goal. Our favourite song for this show was, "In the Air Tonight", a song by Phil Collins. It fitted perfectly to our movements and style of dancing. We would always get table dances together or separately after our show.

Terrifying Accident

One night after my shift I was suppose to meet Jessie at the club where she was working. I ended up in a scary car accident with one of the regular customers from the club I was working at.

This guy would sit at the bar and talk with me in between my sets. He wasn't my customer, just a regular customer who knew the people who ran the bar. There were guys like that. They weren't your customers but you would sit, drink and have conversations with them. This guy wanted to date me.

On this particular night, I told him I had to meet my friend, so he offered to drive me to the club. So, we left. Not too long after we left the club we had an accident. He lost control of the car and ended up running off the road and slamming into the side of a bridge. Thank God we did not breakthrough the barrier. I remember coming out of the car and looking over the bridge into the deep, dark, water below. I was thinking "My God we could have landed in that!" It scared me. What scared me the most was when he told me he would have to leave the car behind because he had been drinking, and to my surprise, he was high on drugs! He said it wouldn't be good for him to be found in that condition by the police. So, we got in a taxi and left the car there.

I was really upset at myself for not having been more careful. I thought he was alright. To be honest, I knew that wasn't the first time I had driven around town with people who were high or drunk. They just knew how to hide it well.

I felt sorry for him. He was upset about the damage to his car. It was a nice car. We met up with Jessie, and later I spent the night with him. When I look back on those times I see how I placed myself in dangerous situations. Someone must have been praying, or looking out for me.

Returning Home

Time went by. Weeks turned into months and months into a few years. I was getting tired of moving around from week to week, and I wanted to go back home. I decided to go to my parent's house during the day, hoping no one would be home. I still had my key, so I let myself in. Everyone was gone, except Grandma. She was surprised to see me. We spoke briefly, nothing in great detail, small talk really. It was so good to see her, and it felt good to be home. It was like being in luxury after going from motel to motel.

I went into my room. The first thing I wanted to do was to take a shower. Afterwards, I went to my room and slept. I woke up to sounds of the family being home, all except Daddy. I went downstairs to see Momma and Deirdre. I knew Grandma would have told them about my return home. As with Grandma, I could tell by their reactions that Momma and Deirdre were surprised that I was home. I wasn't ready to give up any information about what had taken place since I left home, and I could tell they weren't sure what they should ask about. They caught me up to speed on some things I had missed out on about our family and friends.

I stayed in my room for the rest of the night. I knew Momma would let Daddy know I was home. The next day, I saw Daddy. We were polite with one another, but we didn't get into deep conversation. He was very quiet, not the way I left him. Daddy had changed. I knew he was glad I was home. The following days felt like we were adjusting to me being home again. It was a process, but I was elated not to spend another week in a motel room.

Jessie remained "out there", but we would still hang out. One night, I went to meet her and a friend she knew since childhood. Her friend would meet us at the club, while I had to meet Jessie at her new place; she had gotten a room in a rooming house.

I found the rooming house that was located in Hull. The girl who answered the door was very skinny with bulging eyes. She made me feel weak just looking at her because of how skinny she was. I asked for Jessie. I remember as I entered the house I could smell an odour that was extremely strong. It seemed familiar. She pointed to Jessie's room. I knocked. When Jessie came to door I went into her room and asked what the scent was. She said it was from a few of them who liked to sniff glue. As we were leaving there was a guy passing by her room sniffing the glue from what looked like a sandwich bag. It was quite a sight. I told Jessie "Let's go", because the scent was giving me a headache, plus the people going back and forth appeared to be out of it.

Occasionally, we would go out to a few of the clubs in Hull. That night we were going to a gay bar, where Jessie and Veronica had been to before. They thought it was fun to try and get a gay guy to sleep with them. The bar was beyond lively! It was all very new to me; it was a new world to see people of the same sex dancing together and being intimate together. After meeting up with Veronica we decided to take acid. The atmosphere and being on acid was a interesting combination. We mostly stuck with each other, but if someone asked us to dance we did. We spent time pointing out things that seemed amusing. We laughed and danced all over the place. We were having a good time. At one point this girl asked me to dance; it was a fast song so it didn't faze me. The next day, I thought, "What a night!" It was a different world.

Crossing Boundaries

One night, after getting high Jessie and I experimented being intimate with one another. No matter how high I was, I was aware that this didn't seem right. I kept thinking, "This is my best friend" "She is like a sister to me, and we were crossing some boundaries". After awhile we stopped. Maybe we were both thinking the same thing. We both felt strange and after talking about it we came to the same conclusion that it wasn't for us. That was my first experience being sexual with someone of the same sex, but it wouldn't be my last.

My next experience would come later on, when I would share a motel room with a dancer named Isabelle from Montreal. We were both working at the same club in Hull. After we had finished working on the same shift we went back to our motel room. Isabelle asked me if I wanted to do a line of coke. I had heard and seen cocaine in the clubs, but had never tried it before. I knew girls who seemed to live on it. I would see them in the changing room taking turns. I asked Isabelle about it. I wanted to know about its effects. She said it would make me feel sensational. I decided to try it.

She took out a paper from her purse and started to unfold it. It contained a white substance. She emptied it on a mirror, which she also took out of her purse. Isabelle then took out what look like a credit card and started to do chopping motions with the coke on the mirror until she was content with the result. She then parted the coke into lines. There were six of them. She proceeded to take out a paper bill and rolled it up. Isabelle inhaled the white substance through the neatly folded bill. She handed the bill to me. I too inhaled the coke through the bill. Minutes later I had a numbing feeling in my nose and felt like it was dripping in the back of my throat. My heart rate seemed to have quickened. I felt like I was talking a lot. I felt energetic. We took turns inhaling the rest of the lines that were laid out. We started talking about our lives at the clubs, and then we started complimenting each other on our dancing, and each other's bodies. This conversation would lead to us having a sexual encounter.

Being high on coke made me act out in a way I never knew was in me. I did feel sensational. I felt out of control, and aggressive.

Later, I found out that coke or "blow", as it's sometimes called could be snorted, inhaled or injected into your veins. You could smoke it in a joint with Marijuana or hash. Snorting gave you instantaneous, fast acting effects. It caused a feeling of euphoria or being "high." It also elevated your mood, and leaves you feeling energetic and alert.

That would be the last time I would allow myself to have an experience with someone from the same sex. I didn't see Isabelle much after that night. I was relieved that we were not on the same shifts, and if we were, she stayed behind, or went out, and vice versa. I felt uncomfortable being around her, and wanted to avoid her. I was happy when it came to the end of our workweek. Both experiences of being with someone of the same-sex were not something that made me feel good about myself. I felt embarrassed, almost questioning myself. Over the years, I would come across a lot of girls who were either lesbians or bi-sexual. With some girls there was no telling whom they were interested in, unless you spoke to them. Then there were those girls who had no problem in letting you know verbally or physically that they were interested.

After those incidents I couldn't help thinking how innocent I was before leaving home. But then there

I was, making out with my friend, high on drugs, going to places I would never dreamt of going, and hanging out with all kinds of people. I had lost my innocence. It no longer existed. I had changed.

CHAPTER FIVE

Changes

M oving back home was good in the beginning, but soon I got bored. I wasn't going to school or working. It felt like I was taking a break or on vacation from the reality of my life. I actually missed some parts of the club life, especially the money.

I decided to get myself booked in one of the clubs, while I was still at home. I had told my family that I was working in a club as a waitress.

One of the options that I had was to stay at a club working steady as a house girl. If the manager liked you and you were good to look at, and able to do a good set, they didn't mind you working there for a while. At least it allowed you to have a steady paycheque each week. It could be an advantage, because you got familiar with the customers, which was good if one, or more, became regulars for you to make money off them. It could also be a disadvantage if they got bored with seeing you week after week. So, you had to keep things fresh and interesting to keep their attention. I have seen girls who I thought should have stopped dancing years before. I never wanted to end up in the business that long.

Shadiest Characters

It was at this club that I learned a lot about the wheeling and dealings of the underground world. The shadiest people entered the doors of most of the clubs, but this one club in particular seemed to have the greatest in number. It was here that I was introduced to a lot of things. At this club I met the girl who was dating one of the bartenders; she knew how to get peoples credit cards in advance before they did. She would be able to purchase you anything you wanted at her own rate of course, but you had to pay her in cash. I was surprised she never got arrested for fraud. There were the bikers from the Outlaw chapter, a prominent biker group; their rivals were the Hell's Angels. It was a known fact that Police detectives were always sitting outside of this club. Through the years I worked with quite a few dancers who were biker chicks. One thing with the bikers, as I was warned, if you dated one of its member you would have the groups protection, but he also would share you with the rest of the other members. My physique was what attracted them. They thought I was a body builder. I was getting very muscular, especially in my thighs, arms and upper back. When I walked it felt like I was carry a tonne, but it made me feel very strong.

A New Relationship

It was while working at this club that I met the guy I would spend many years of my life with. He was like a son to the club owner, and best friends with one of the owner's sons. They became friends in their early school days, and they continued the relationship into adulthood. They seemed to have a lot in common.

I noticed him whenever he came into the club. At times I would notice him paying attention to me while I did my set. He wasn't usually in the area where the dancers were. He spent most of his time with his friends in the pool hall area. He was tall with fair skin, dark hair, green eyes, and handsome, the jock type.

One night, he finally approached me. We started talking. His name was Jake. After a few nights of conversations he asked me out. We went out to a very nice restaurant that night, and had a great time in deep conversation. We learned a lot about each other. I could tell he was very smart, knowledgeable about things and life, which I liked. Another thing I liked about him was that he was athletic. He was into a lot of sports. His main sports were hockey and football. We were very open and comfortable with each other. He was very different from the guys I had come across previously.

Jake would meet me at work and we would go to his apartment. We were seeing a lot of each other and having fun. He wined and dined me after my shifts at work, and it felt good to have that kind of attention. He was a very good cook. I spent more time at his place than my parents, and eventually it became my home too. I still went to my parent's home, but not as much.

While we were dating, and eventually living together, I became aware that there was another side to him. Jake and his friends sold drugs, but I didn't pay too much attention to it. It was part of both our worlds. Sometimes he would have marijuana, also called pot, or weed. It was a green brown grey mixture of dried, shredded leaves, stem and seeds. I hated the smell of it. Most of the time Jake, would have a large chunk of hashish, or hash, as we would call it. It was dark-coloured, sticky and thick and contained the same active ingredients as marijuana, but in a higher concentration. Later on I would see it in oil form.

I knew where Jake hid his hash when he had it. If I didn't know where it was, I would go hunting for it until I found it. I would take pieces off and bring it to work and give to the girls, or I would smoke up with them. I liked smoking hash. It made me feel very relaxed almost sedated. I wasn't into getting high while I was working at first, but slowly I didn't mind it as much, especially if it was a slow day or night.

They say all good things must come to an end. Well, my relationship with Jake almost did after some months of seeing each other. Sometimes in his wheeling and dealings, Jake would end up around all sorts of people, which concerned me, especially when I got home and he wasn't there. I used to worry that maybe he had gotten arrested.

Jake used to hang out with this one particular guy. He was one of the bartenders at the club I worked. They partnered up in going out to clubs and pubs where they met with people to do deals. I hated it. It made me nervous.

Unfaithful

One night while they were out, they ended up at a house party. Jake didn't come home. I was very worried, that something bad happened to him. The next day he showed up full of apologies and smelling like he needed to spend some time in the shower. He told me he had gotten high and drunk at a party. He also mentioned that he had slept with one of the girls at the party who turned out to be a dancer. I knew her. She had worked at the same club as I did. She was an older dancer compared to me with a British accent. His explanation was that they were both high and drunk. After some weeks went by, Jake told me that she was pregnant. It was distressing news, but we found out that it was an ectopic pregnancy also known as tubal pregnancy. This form of pregnancy is when the fertilized egg attaches somewhere other than the uterus, most often it's in the fallopian tube. As it was an abnormal pregnancy, she had to receive treatment to end it.

The whole situation was devastating to me. It shocked me that he would have cheated on me. I thought our relationship was going so well. I wasn't about to continue a relationship with someone who cheated on me. Jake pleaded and apologized and tried very hard to make up for what he said was a really bad mistake. I felt he was sincere, and I did believe him, but it took me a very long time to move on from this experience. I felt betrayed and hurt. I found the whole situation painful. I hated the way it made me feel. There were other people who knew what had taken place, which only added more pain and drama. I forgave him. We continued with our relationship. I didn't realize it at the time, but his actions would destroy any commitment or trust that was between us, or could have developed in the relationship in the years that we would spend together.

As time went by I started drinking more, most of the time with Jake. Sometimes I would drink with my customers. I drank liqueurs mostly. Grand Marnier was my favourite or white wine. Red wine always gave me a headache; people used to say it was because it had more sugar. Having a couple of drinks always made me feel good, in the mood, especially when I had to do table dances. It helped me feel more seductive, sensual, and friendlier towards the customers. I was beginning to really understand why most of the girls drank or got high. It helped.

Moving Away

One night after my shift, I went home to some surprising news. Jake informed me that he had been accepted to a university in Montreal. He would have to leave shortly to begin training camp; he was accepted to play football for them, which he was very excited about. He wasn't sure if he would have gotten accepted; therefore he never said anything beforehand, in case things didn't work out.

I was very surprised! All I thought about was that he was moving away and leaving me. What was more surprising was that Jake asked me to move to Montreal with him. I wasn't sure about that. Even though I had moved in with him and was spending most of my time with him, the thought of moving away from my family again scared me. I was not ready to have this relationship end either, so I agreed to move with Jake to Montreal.

We went in advance to check out some apartments. After looking at a few, we finally decided on an apartment in Ville St Pierre. It was in an older neighbourhood. Some of the buildings on the outside looked unkempt, like no one had been taking care of them for years. I felt our building at anytime could fall over, but our time frame was short. I knew I could dress it up to be a comfortable place for us to live just like I had done at our first apartment.

I took some time off from dancing while we packed up and moved, and spent some more time setting up our new home. I knew I would be able to get bookings in Ottawa as a dancer from out of town, which is what I did. I would be able to stay at the motel where the dancers stayed.

A Night of Intimidation

I worked for a while doing a circuit of Fabian's clubs and went back to the club where I worked as a house girl. One evening after my shift Jessie and I met up. She was with a young guy she had met while working in one of the clubs. He wasn't the type I usually saw her with. He was a few years younger than we were. I had never met him before, but she had mentioned him in conversations over the phone, how young he was, and that he was infatuated with her. We went back to my motel room, which was provided by the club, to hang out.

A few hours later while hanging out in my room, there was a knock at my door, to my surprise it was Terrance, a guy Jessie met some time back while she was working at the same club I was now working at. To me he was a wannabe biker. He usually hung out at the club. Terrance always seemed to have a large black Rottweiler with him. There were rumours about him and his dog, but I won't go into that. After he barged in uninvited, he wanted to know what was going on and who the young guy was. Terrance wasn't pleased at all that Jessie was with this guy, so he spent some time in my room being upset and threatening to let his dog loose on us. We were all afraid of what he and his dog would do. After what seemed like a very long time of us begging him to leave us alone, he left feeling proud that he had frightened us. I told Jake about what happened that night. It came at no surprise to later hear that Terrance was "dealt" with. I wasn't given any details of what had occurred, nor did I ask.

It was at those times that I realized that Jessie's taste in the male persuasion was something I would never figure out. During the times that we worked, traveled, and clubbed together, I was always the one looking out for her. I was known as the not so friendly one, which was fine by me. I learned quickly when we started out, that the industry we were in wasn't such a friendly one if you came across the wrong guy. My guard had to be up at all times, even when it turned out that it didn't need to be. When

I look back, it was this defence mechanism that saved me from being raped and taken advantage of on quite a few occasions.

One incident happened when Jessie met a guy who owned a motorcycle. She was crazy about motorcycles. He asked her if she wanted a ride, and of course, she said "Yes!" She went for a ride with him, while I waited outside for them to return. When they did return Jessie didn't seem herself. The guy asked me if I wanted a turn. I said "No thanks". Then he left. After he left Jessie told me that he brought her to a secluded place and tried to rape her. I was livid with her for not saying anything, and thought "What if I would have gone with him?" I'm sure; he would have tried the same thing with me. She said she figured I wouldn't have gone with him anyways. My lack of trust in men and their motives grew more and more. It stemmed from the fact that all they wanted was sex, in one way or another.

Jessie eventually met a guy who lived in Hull. He was nice. He seemed more "normal" than any of the guys she had ever introduced me to. She moved in with him after a short period of time and was in a happy place. Jake and I spent time with them when he was in town. After awhile we stopped staying in touch. Our lives were changing and we saw less and less of each other. Jessie dropped out of my life.

I started to get tired of the club life after awhile. I was looking to settle down and have a normal life.

CHAPTER SIX

The "Normal" Life

After my twenty-first birthday, I felt like I didn't have much going on in my life. I was working, but I felt I was going through the motions as though I had nothing meaningful in my life. I came across girls who had kids and were so happy when they spoke about them. I thought they had a purpose, a reason to be working, and put up with all that went with the job. I spoke to Jake about wanting a baby. I thought it would make me happy and fulfill me. I felt that was what I needed. So, I went to see my family doctor and asked her about going through the process to get off the pill, so I could get pregnant. She told me at which point I would need to be off the pill in order to have a safe pregnancy. I filled Jake in on the doctor's recommendations. We decided that I would come off the pill, and see what would happen.

I Am Pregnant

One day, while I was in the kitchen at my parent's house, Momma was cooking. I started to complain about the smell of the food, this wasn't the first time. It was suggested that I should go and see our doctor, as I might be pregnant. After I visited the doctor, I got the results, and sure enough I was pregnant! It had taken a short period of time after following the doctor's recommendations before I became pregnant.

I was weeks into my pregnancy; surprised, overjoyed, and elated! I couldn't believe something so wonderful had happened to me. I called Jake to share the good news. He was very surprised. He thought it would have taken longer for me to get pregnant. I knew he wasn't too sure about us having a baby so soon, because of course we were both so young. I was only twenty-one and he was just a couple of years older and in University. I already knew if I had to go it alone, then I would do what I had to do. I wanted this baby. Thank God, Jake got over the shock. It didn't last too long. He was on board and we were going on this journey together.

As soon as I found out I was pregnant I stopped everything that I thought would, or could harm the baby that was growing inside of me. There was no more drinking, or doing drugs. I worked until I was three months into my pregnancy, and then I was out of the business. I wasn't sure what I was going to do for money. Jake reassured me that things would work out.

Right away I went out and got my first baby book. I wanted to know what was going on inside of me. I needed to know all the details. This book was like a best friend with a lot of answers. I looked forward to each stage of my pregnancy.

During my pregnancy, I would go back and forth from Montreal to Ottawa, because my doctor was still in Ottawa. In the early stages of my pregnancy I started to have sharp pains in my abdomen. So, I made an appointment to see my doctor right a way for fear that something was wrong. What my doctor had to say wasn't what I was prepared to hear. She told me that sometimes in the early stages; it is possible to have a miscarriage. I'm not sure what else she said after that. I tuned her out, and fear gripped me. The thought of losing the baby was something that scared me. I left my appointment, and called Jake who was in Montreal. He was unable to come with me on this visit. I told him what the doctor had said. He was very encouraging and told me not to worry. He assured me that everything would be fine. I felt better after speaking to him. He always had a way of making me feel better. I found myself saying a little prayer for everything to be alright with my pregnancy. I made sure to stop and pick up the vitamins my doctor had prescribed, still in a bit of a daze from our conversation. I decided from that day I was going to do everything to make sure I had the baby, but most importantly a healthy baby. As I entered my fourth trimester I felt a lot better. I felt more reassure that things were going to be alright.

Panic Attack

Further on into my pregnancy, I had a frightful experience. I was in Montreal and had said goodbye to Jake, who was going off to his class. I got into a phone booth to call back home to touch base with my parents. After speaking to Momma I got off the phone. Suddenly, I had no idea where I was. I couldn't remember why or how I got there. I panicked! My heart was racing so fast. I felt faint, and dizzy. I was sweating profusely. I was having problems catching my breath. I got out of the phone booth not knowing where to go. My eyes landed on a nearby grocery store. I went in. There was a lady and an older gentleman by the counter. I told them something was wrong with me, still panicking. I was in tears now. They were asking me questions, which I couldn't answer. I had no recollection of anything before entering that phone booth. They had me sit down and gave me some water trying to calm me down. I calmed down and sat quietly for a bit. Then it was as if the moment had lifted. I felt as though I was coming out of a bad dream. Things were starting to make sense. I slowly began to remember where I was and how I ended up there. I told them I didn't live far from the store and was going to go straight home. I thank them for their help. I was so happy to be back to myself. It was a scary moment. I was told later that it seemed I had had a panic attack. Fortunately, after that scare, the rest of my pregnancy was a wonderful experience. I enjoyed being pregnant watching my belly grow and feeling the baby moving around inside of me. It was an amazing thing to experience.

I went through odd cravings. I usually craved fine smooth dirt. I am not sure why. My biggest craving, though, was fresh snow. When the craving came on, I would watch Jake go outside and try to retrieve a glass of fresh snow. It was the best thing at that moment. We were excited and getting anxious to see our baby. It was a joy buying and collecting baby items. As I got closer to my due date travelling became tiresome. We decided it was best for me to stay at my parent's home. Jake came as often as he could get away. Because we were not married we were not allowed to sleep in the same bed even though I was pregnant, so whenever Jake was able to come he had to sleep on the pull out couch in the basement. We thought this was funny, but it was my parent's house, and their rules, which we understood, and respected.

We never knew the sex of our baby in advance. My doctor said she wouldn't do an ultrasound for the purpose of knowing the sex of the baby. She would only do one if she suspected there was something wrong with the baby. It wasn't such a big deal to know, not like it is today. We received beautiful gifts for our baby from the baby shower my family held. The colours of the items were neutral.

Baby on the Way

One night after going to the bathroom I wiped myself, and noticed that there was discharge of blood and mucus on the toilet paper. I wasn't too alarmed because I remembered reading that that was one of the signs of labour. It was called "show". I hurried downstairs to let Jake know what was happening. He was staying with me until after the baby was born. He called the doctor who asked to be kept posted on how I was progressing. I no longer had my family doctor taking care of me. Her area of specialization didn't include the delivery of babies. She temporarily connected me with another doctor who specialized in delivery.

I stayed downstairs with Jake, still excited. We talked for a while, and then decided to play cards. We were anxiously watching and waiting for the time to speed up. As time went on, I kept feeling pressure and pain in my lower back along with painful cramps in my abdomen. I felt like I was having my period, but with more intense pain. The pain started to intensify. I hated, and despise that pain. When it came it seemed to shock my body. I felt as though I couldn't breathe and think at the same time. I was relieved when Jake called the doctor and he said it was ok to head to the hospital. It was early morning outside.

I was relieved to be at the hospital, I felt safe there. They checked my cervix and told us how far I was dilated. I had already decided ahead of time that I would take the epidural. It was a choice I made. I was concerned about the report that it may paralyse me, or that I may experience severe back pain later on in life. To administer the epidural anaesthetic are passed into the small of your back via a fine tube. The drug is injected around the nerves that carry signals from the part of your body that feels pain when you're in labour.

I knew when the time came there was no way I was going to be brave enough and endure the pain. I felt like the pain was going to kill me before I delivered our baby. I was wheeled into a room and two nurses attended to me. One was instructing me and holding me still. The other was behind me setting up the epidural. I remember feeling something entering my back that caused a sharp pain. It felt as though it was a contraction. It was so painful, but after the epidural it was smooth sailing. The nurses would tell me when I was having a contraction, and I would smile and say "Oh really!"

We weren't in the delivery room for long before I was following instructions to push. I was happy Jake was by my side. After I had pushed for a short time the doctor decided forceps was needed to help guide our baby through the birth canal. The forceps were an instrument that resembled a pair of tongs. I had concerns about this cause I had read that some babies came out with the imprint from the forceps on their foreheads, but I wanted them to do whatever it would take to get the baby out safely.

Finally, right before seven in the morning, the baby we had been waiting for, cried out. Our baby girl was finally here! When they announced it was a girl I was elated. I had prayed to God to let our baby be a girl. I wanted to have a little me. Someone I would love and take care of. I wanted to dress her up and do her hair, and all the other things that make some women want to have a little girl. I felt God had answered my prayer.

Medical Issues

Unfortunately, that moment of joy wouldn't last too long. After holding our baby for a short time; they took her away quickly, and were busy attending to me. I was hooked up to a bag from which blood was coming from. I was wheeled out of the delivery room to another part of the hospital. I felt as though I was drifting away. At that moment I started to pray. I had no idea what was happening. I said "God, you gave me a girl, please don't take me away from her." I never forgot that moment, or what I said.

Later, Jake explained to me that I had been hae-morrhaging, which meant after our baby came out

I started to bleed fast and uncontrollable. I lost a lot of blood. I had to receive two bags of blood. I also had a yellow discoloration of the skin, called Jaundice. It had a lot to do with the breakdown or destruction of red blood cells. In addition to this, I got torn in the process of delivery. I experienced vaginal pain way after the painkillers had worn off. But all this didn't take away from my happiness that at the age of twenty-one I had become a mother.

When I saw our daughter again, I noticed right away that she had a splint on her left hand. The doctor said that our daughter had been injured during the delivery. Without the splint her hand would drop down. It wouldn't stay up on its own. He assured us that there was no cause for alarm, and with the help of the splint her hand would be back to normal in no time.

Besides that she was a beautiful baby with chubby cheeks fair skin and greenish blue eyes. She was so calm. Her eyes seemed to be taking in her new atmosphere. I thought she bore a striking resemblance to Jake. Because we didn't know the sex of our baby in advance we had picked names for both a boy and a girl. When we were asked to give her name for the paperwork, we were delighted to give them her names. I felt they suited her perfectly.

Momma popped into my room before she went off to work. Throughout the day we had visitors stopping by to congratulate us on our new bundle of joy. Later that night I felt something swoosh out of me. When I touched it, it reminded me of liver. I was afraid of what it could be. I buzzed for the nurse, who came right away, and put me at ease. She said it was part of my placenta. The placenta, also known as afterbirth, was connecting my baby to my uterus. The nurse wrapped it up and took it away.

Before giving birth I had decided previously that I would not be breastfeeding. Some of the dancers advised that "If I knew I was going back to dancing, it was best not to breastfeed because of what it could do to my breasts". I saw girls who had breastfed babies and had gone back to dancing. Their breasts had lost their perkiness, and I didn't want my breast to sag like that. It was a decision I wrestled with, but once I made it I stuck with it. Later there were times I did wonder if I had made the right decision. I heard other mothers voicing their opinions on the importance of breastfeeding and the bond that it created between mother and baby. But it worked out for me. I never felt there wasn't a bond between Cassie and I. Therefore I never regretted my decision.

After spending a couple of days in the hospital I went back to my parent's house. I felt tired when I got there. Cassie was sleeping, so I went to lay down for a nap myself. I began to feel hot and my breasts where hurting, my back too. When I felt my breasts, they were huge, and hard as a rock. The only thing I could compare them to were the breasts of the country singer, Dolly Parton. Jake called the doctor. It turned out that I should have gotten a pre-scription to dry up the milk that I would be producing since I wasn't going to breastfeed. The pain was intense. Jake rushed out and got the prescription. When I got the pills I finally got some relief. The dif-ference I felt was like night and day.

Ten days after giving birth to Cassie, which was the best early birthday present, it was my twen-ty-second birthday. Jake and I decided to go out. It was the first time we had been out together since Cassie's birth. We went by the club where I was a house girl, the place where Jake and I first met. That's where our friends hung out. They were happy to see us, and full of congratulations. Even though it was the first time I had left Cassie behind I knew she would be in good hands with Momma and Deirdre.

A few days after my birthday we headed back to our home in Montreal. We had moved into a nicer neighbourhood during my pregnancy, because I hated our first apartment. Our neighbours all seemed sketchy to me. One weekend while we were away, in Ottawa, we were robbed. Amongst some of the items that were stolen were a white rabbit fur coat, and some jewellery Jake had bought me. I was very upset. Later, Jake found out that one of our neighbours was involved in us being robbed. "He got what was coming to him", was all that was said. I asked no questions. I knew payback was given. We moved not too long after that incident.

It was nice being in my own home again. I had to find a doctor for Cassie immediately. I was happy when her splint was removed. Her wrist was perfectly normal. It was an adjustment for us having a baby. The late nights and early morning feedings were something we had to get use to. But we were enjoying being parents. The days, however, were very long and tiresome after a while.

Homesick and Lonely

Months later, with Jake still in university, playing football, and working, I became lonely. He would try to pop in when he could throughout the day, but when he had to leave it left me feeling even lonelier. At times I saw him in the morning and not again until late at night when he returned home. We lived across from a friendly lady in our basement apartment. She was always locked up in her apartment with her cat, and a heavy smoker. Her curtains were always drawn, which left her apartment stuffy and dark; therefore I didn't go to her place often. There was another young lady upstairs from us with a little girl, but we saw each other once in a while. It was becoming too hard being alone in Montreal. I missed my family. I knew they would be a good support for me and Cassie if we were closer. Momma and Deirdre came to visit on separate occasions. But it wasn't the same as being in the same town. I was always sad when they had to go. I was home-sick. I didn't want to disrupt or burden Jake while he was getting a better education. So, after discussing it with him, I packed up and moved back to Ottawa. Cassie was six months old at the time. Jake moved in with some of the guys from the university and stayed to continue his schooling.

I stayed at my parent's home for a short period until I was able to get my own place. I knew I wasn't ready to go back to work as yet. I had to put aside by pride and seek financial help from the govern-ment. I was willing to do whatever it took to spend time to take care of Cassie. After being qualified to receive financial help I found a place about twenty minutes from my parent's home by bus. I was glad to be back in the city that was home. I felt more comfortable.

My contentment didn't last long. I started to feel depressed and lonely. I didn't see anyone except my family. I had no friends I felt I could relate to. Jake came as often as he could. It was wonderful when we were together, but most of the time I felt as though I was a single mother living on my own.

During one of my visits to my parent's home I ran into a guy that I use to know. He lived a few doors down from my parents' place. He was a few years younger than me but we had fun and started hanging out. I would go by his house when I dropped by my parents with Cassie. Sometimes he came to my apartment after I had put Cassie to bed. We usually drank and got high together. Eventually, I ended up sleeping with him. This went on for a period of time. It didn't mean anything. It was filling in the gap, but it made me feel horrible about myself, so I ended it.

I started to drink on my own; not too much because of Cassie, but just enough to make me feel good. At times, when Jake came into town he would leave me a couple of joints of hash or marijuana.

Emotional Meltdown

One day while I was at my parent's home, I had a few drinks. I would sneak Daddy's liquor at times. I never wanted my parents to know how much I was drinking and I definitely didn't want them to know I was taking drugs. Deirdre was home downstairs watching TV and Cassie was sleeping. I went upstairs and turned on the TV in Momma's room since Cassie was asleep in my old room. Oprah was on. The topic was about molestation. I was sitting there listening to the stories of individuals who had been molested, and all of a sudden I became emotional. I found myself having flashbacks about the first time I was molested, then the second time. I had a meltdown. All I could think about was the need to tell Momma. In tears, I fumbled around in search for the number for the hospital where Momma worked. Finally, I found the number, and when I heard Momma's voice on the phone I let it all out. I was crying like a baby. I was wailing. Through all the crying I could here her questions "What?" "Why would he do that?" She said she would talk to me more when she came home. Hours later Momma came home. I was still in her room as I had fallen asleep in her bed. I woke up hearing her enter the room. I had a headache. We spoke briefly. I didn't want to talk about the molestation. I was sorry I had called her and blurted out what was locked up inside of me for years. I rushed out of the room to see Cassie. Deirdre was looking after her. We never spoke about it after that night.

Fighting Suicidal Thoughts

I started to sink deeper into depression after this incident. I was having thoughts of suicide on a regular basis. I wanted out of this life. I was consumed by how I should end my life. I also thought about Cassie. She was almost one year old. I felt she would be better off without me, because I wasn't in the state of mind to be a good mother. I knew she would be well taken care of by Jake and my family.

One day feeling distressed and contemplating how I could end my life. Suddenly, my thoughts went to calling Fabian, to ask him for a job. Fabian was the owner of most of the strip clubs in Ottawa, and some in Hull. I'm not sure why he came to my mind, because I didn't know him very well. Sometimes our path crossed in the clubs, and we said hello to each other, but nothing more.

I remembered that Fabian spent most of his time at one particular club. I searched for the club's number and called him, not sure what I was going to say. A female answered the phone. After asking for Fabian I was placed on hold. I could here loud music playing in the background. I thought about what I should say. Finally, I heard a man's voice saying "Hello this is Fabian." I said, "Hello" and began explaining to him that I used to work for his agency, and I was looking for a job, but not as a dancer. I asked if there were any waitressing positions available in any of his clubs. I knew it would be no problem since I worked as a waitress previously. He said, "Sorry, but there are no openings at the moment for a waitress". However, he did say that I could work in the coatroom checking coats at one of his clubs in Hull. This particular club was fairly new, and was for male dancers. It was located above the club for female dancers.

I was surprised at the offer, but said yes to the position. Fabian said I could start later in the week. I thanked him and hung up the phone. I was ecstatic. I was going to start working again and it had nothing to do with me taking my clothes off. It was a normal job. The day couldn't come soon enough. For the moment my thoughts of suicide passed.

A New Direction

I told my family about my new job and that I needed their help in watching Cassie when I had to work. They were willing to help me out, as always.

The day came to start my new job. After dropping Cassie off at my parents' home I took a taxi and headed to the club. The taxi pulled up at the building where the club was located. I got out and walked towards the door. I could here loud music coming from the club. It was the club located downstairs with the female dancers. I then saw the doors for the male dancers. I took the stairs that lead up to the club. At the entrance there was an Asian guy. He was slim, and didn't have the physique of the bouncers that I was used to seeing at the doors. He acknowledged me and I told him that I was there to see Fabian. He pointed to the back of the club where the office was located. The music was loud as usual. There were female customers and quite a number of male dancers. It was a scene I hadn't seen for a long time. It felt different being in a club again.

I worked my way through the crowd feeling a bit nervous now that I was there. I found the office and knocked at the door. A man in his thirties with black slicked back hair, dressed in a nice suit came to the door. I asked for Fabian and was lead inside. There he was, sitting at a desk, just the way that I remembered him. I introduced myself. I was sure he probably had no idea who I was. If he had known who I was, he certainly didn't act like it. He introduced me to the man who opened the door. His name was Serge. He was the club's manager. I always liked Fabian. He was Italian, in his late forties to early fifties. He was an older distinguish man. I thought he was a gentleman. He was always nicely dressed, but humble. He was quiet in nature, but friendly. Over the years, whenever I saw Fabian, he was never loud or vulgar, but it was obvious, that he was in charge, a businessman, and he owned things.

We had a good conversation about my life since I left the club life. He caught me up to speed as to the changes and additions in the clubs. He told me my wage and work schedule, which was Thursdays to Saturdays seven in the evening until three in the morning. It was the busier time for the club.

Fabian had Serge introduce me to the doorman. His name was Bing. He gave me the information on my job requirements, which sounded pretty straightforward. My job was to take each coat as the customers came in. There was a roll of tickets, which had two parts. One part was placed on the hanger with the coat, and the other part went to the customer to show when retrieving their coat later. There was a fee required to check your coat. It was more mandatory than necessary. The coatroom was a large room that reminded me of a walk-in closet. There was a glass container located on the counter that had the word "tip" written on it. Serge left Bing and I, and went back to the office. Prior to me working there, Bing had to check the coats and also kept a counter in his hand to keep track of the number of people who visited the club. I was required to use a cash register, and would be given a certain amount of money to start each shift.

The club was set up so that everything was within view. It was an extremely nice club. It had a dance floor on the left side, and a bar, which was well laid out on the right. The stage for the dancers was also located on the left side. It was evident it was a new club. Fabian came by a few hours later to say he was leaving for the night, and that Serge would take care of me. I thanked him again for giving me the job.

The night went by smoothly. During my shift some of the dancers came by to introduce themselves. I found the dancers very friendly. The ladies were also nice to me. They were all dressed up and looking good. They weren't reluctant to leave tips when they left, which were divided between Bing and I at the end of the night.

At the end of the night I was introduced to William, the bartender. He was also Asian. I liked him. He reminded me of a comical big brother. I found out that William didn't live too far from my home in Ottawa, and he offered me a ride home, which I was thankful for. It was good to be out again.

Things were going well. I was getting into a routine, taking care of Cassie during the days. Towards the end of the week I worked at the club. It was a very busy club on the weekends. Once again I was in a club with screaming ladies, but I didn't mind. I was happy to be out working. I saw some of the dancers I had worked with in the past. I was getting familiar with the regular customers, and even the police officers that popped in to check on things. One particular officer often engaged me in conversation. I liked him. On one of his visits he suggested that we go out on a date, but with our schedules it never happened.

High Class Escorts

There was a particular group of ladies that were regulars. When they showed up; they always got the attention of the dancers. They gravitated to their table. These ladies spent a lot of money on table dancing and buying bottles of Dom Pérignon. I was very familiar with it from my days of working in the clubs. It is very expensive, and popular with the customers with lots of money. I found out from

Bing that the ladies were high priced escorts. They were always dressed fancy, and extremely friendly. I liked them. The leader of the group was a good-looking black lady, and the others were white. Two of the ladies were sisters, and were very pretty; the youngest sister had eyes that reminded me of a Siberian husky. I don't usually come across someone with eyes like that. They were a fun group when they showed up.

The ladies were there one night after my shift. Most of the time they stayed until the club closed. They invited me to their house, which they all shared together. Since it was a Saturday night, I agreed to go. Their house was located close to the club. It was spacious and nicely decorated. Some of the male and female dancers arrived there shortly after. The next thing I knew, it was a vibrant party. There was lots of drinking. Then, I noticed the mirror along with the rolled up bill being passed around. A sight I was familiar with. I took my turn and inhaled the coke, and passed it along. I was wide awake considering I had had such a long day, and surprisingly I wasn't hungry. I liked how I felt on coke. Through out my time there the mirror seemed as if it was continuously being passed around. There was lots of conversation going on around me. Eventually, I got tired and the next thing I knew it was bright outside. It was morning. Some people had fallen asleep beside me, and some were still talking away. All I was thinking about was the need for me to get home. I got someone to call me a taxi and I went home. I got home and went straight to bed.

I never went back to the escorts' house, but I still hung out with them. Whenever I did there was constant laughter. Some nights after work we would end up at a nearby restaurant. It was open twenty-four hours, and was always packed. It could be very chaotic at times, because it was the only place on the strip that was opened that late, and everyone was hungry after the clubs closed. This is where you found the pimps, the hookers, escorts, dancers, bouncers, drug dealers, drug addicts, and gang members. All sorts hung out at this restaurant after hours.

At times we had to wait until there was a table available. The waiting time could be short or long depending on how busy it was, or who was working at the door that night. It was common to come across someone getting high in the bathroom or who wanted to sell you some form of drugs.

There wasn't a night that someone wasn't getting into a fight, whether it was a boyfriend, and his girlfriend, husband and wife, friends, or total strangers. This would lead to someone getting thrown out, or the police being called. The police were always out in full force on the streets, by the end of the night when the clubs closed. The streets were full of activity. I saw all kinds of drama unfolding around me. It became normal to pass people on the streets that were either trying to pick me up, fighting, crying, or just behaving badly.

I got used to this kind of lifestyle. During this time Jake was still coming back and forth from Montreal to Ottawa. It was very lonely being by myself and going home to an empty apartment.

Border Crossing

One night after work, William invited me along for a ride across to the US border. I found out that was where Serge was from. William was to follow Serge to ensure he got across the border. I wasn't up to going home to an empty apartment as Cassie was at my parent's home, so I agreed to go. I was happy to follow along to avoid my loneliness. A friend of Serge's who I had met before was also going along. I would ride with William in his car, and Serge and his friend would be driving in another car.

We left immediately after work and hit the road. While travelling, William and I had a long conversation about the club life, and about our countries of birth.

I had no idea where we were. We got to a certain area and Serge and his friend said good-bye. I assumed we crossed over the border. They continued to drive in the same direction, but we turned around to go back to Canada. The area was deserted. I didn't see anything around. We started to head back and the next thing I knew, William said we were being followed by one of the Customs officers in a jeep. I immediately became nervous and noticed that William was too. We were pulled over and asked why we didn't stop at the Customs office.

William replied that we were lost. The officer said we needed to come back to the station with him. We were placed in the back of his car and taken to the Customs office. I was more nervous now, and wondering if I was under arrest for something I had no idea about, even though I wasn't in hand-cuffs. All I could think about was how am I going to explain this to my family and Jake.

Once at the station, they separated both of us. I was taken into a room and asked for my passport and ID, which of course I didn't have. I had no ID on me except my social insurance card. I was asked a lot of questions about why we travelled across the border and questions about Serge. They had stopped him also. They wanted to know about the car that he was driving. I had no idea what was going on. I told the officer I worked with them in a club, and I was asked if I wanted to come along for the ride across the border, and that was it. The officer kept leaving the room, and then he would return. Finally, after what seemed like hours, I was given a letter that stipulates that I should not enter the United States for one year. I was relieved that they were letting me go. I saw William waiting when I came out of the room. The officer brought us back to William's car, and we left.

William was as shaken up as I was. He said he was sorry and explained that Serge had wanted to get across the border without paying tax on his car. William was just supposed to follow along in case anything went wrong.

Our ride back to the Canadian border felt very long. I have never been so happy to cross over into Canada. We were both happy. William dropped me off at home and I entered my apartment thinking how things could have turned out otherwise. I was upset at myself for being careless. The next day I told my family what happened. They agreed that it was careless, but they were glad it wasn't worse.

When Serge came back, he apologized to both William and I for what happened at the border. We laughed about the experience. I knew I would never place myself in a situation like that again.

An Evening with Fabian

Working at the club enabled me to see Fabian on a regular basis. We became friendlier with each other. He wasn't married as far as I knew, but while working in the clubs I heard he once had a serious relationship with a black dancer, but something happened and the relationship ended. In our conversations he never spoke about any of his relationships. One night he invited me to his home for dinner the following evening. I said, "Yes". The plan was to meet him at the club, where he would pick me up. I was excited he had asked me to his home for dinner. I liked his personality and enjoyed our conversations.

The next day after dropping Cassie off at my parents' home I took a taxi to the club. Fabian was already there waiting. We left the club as soon as I got there and headed for his home. I asked where he lived; he said his home was located in Aylmer, which wasn't too far from the club. The ride was about twenty to twenty-five minutes.

It felt like we were going out of town, or to the countryside. The lots were large, and the houses too. There was a fair distance between them. We reached our destination, and made our way through a gate, then down a long driveway, that circled in front of the house. His house looked exactly the way I had expected. It was large, and beautiful.

We entered his home, and the inside was also beautiful. He welcomed me to his home, and showed me around; I thought his house reflected him very well. It was classic, from the furniture to the pictures, to the ornaments. A lot of planning went into everything that was laid out in his house. It looked wealthy and vibrant.

He offered me a drink, and I chose to have a glass of white wine. He poured us both a glass, and proceeded to make dinner. It was different to see him like that; I was used to seeing him in the club atmosphere where he was all business. I was still taken aback that I was there in his home, and that he was cooking dinner for us. While he cooked we talked about many different topics. Dinner was finally ready after a period of time, and we sat down to eat. It was delicious! I was surprised that he could cook.

After dinner we settled in the living room in front of a beautiful fireplace. I have always had a thing for fireplaces. We continued to have different conversations, and drink more wine. Fabian leaned over and kissed me, and I returned his kiss. I was happy I was finally alone with him. We left the living room and went to his bedroom to continue what we started. Being with each other felt like it was something we had both been waiting for. It was a very passionate encounter.

Afterwards, we were lying in bed talking, when the phone rang. It was someone from one of the clubs. He spoke to the person briefly, and then said he would be there shortly. He got off the phone and apologized, but said he had to go. Something had happened at one of the clubs, and he had to go. We got dressed and headed back to the club. Fabian got one of the drivers for the dancers to drop me home. He kissed me goodbye and said we would talk the next day. Our evening together had ended.

Fabian and I never spent another evening like that again. We only spent time hanging out at the club when we saw each other. I was never the type of girl who pursued a man, and I wasn't about to start now. Despite how much I may have placed it in the back of my mind, the fact remained that I was still in a relationship with Jake.

Working in the club atmosphere again, and seeing some of the girls I had worked with previously made me want to return to dancing. I missed the amount of money I used to make. What I was making at my new position wasn't even in the same vicinity. I missed being able to buy what I wanted. I found it difficult just getting by on what I was making and I hated being partially on social assistance.

So, after many months of working as a coat check girl, I decided to quit my job and returned to dancing.

Back to the Stage

I called the agency and they got me a booking in one of Fabian's clubs. I was very nervous about returning to the stage. I still had some weight on me from having Cassie, but only those who knew me from before would notice the difference, otherwise you would think that's how I looked. I didn't gain much weight from my pregnancy. People use to say that from the back you couldn't tell I was pregnant. I honestly thought it was because of the dancing why my body bounced back so quickly except for my stomach that was where I saw the effects of having been pregnant. I knew lots of girls who were dancers that had bodies that I thought didn't fit the image of what a dancer looked like. It never stopped them from baring it all. There were ways to camouflage what you didn't feel comfortable showing. It was good to be dancing again not just financially, but it was my social life.

I found out champagne rooms were the big thing. The room was big and private to those who wanted privacy away from the crowds. Sometimes there would be no one in the room but you and your customer and if there were others in the room it didn't matter because everyone was doing their own thing.

The price was higher than a regular table dance, and because the room was dim you were able to dance closer, intimate, and more seductive. Girls were watched by other dancers, waitresses or bouncers who pop their heads in to ensure that no one was crossing any boundaries. If a dancer was in the room for a long period of time, it was assumed that she maybe pushing the boundaries, which wasn't always the case. Some men just got hooked, and reeled in. I have seen men who would leave, and come back. Why? They would go to the bank to withdraw more money to return.

A few of the clubs got renovated. They were much nicer than before. When a new strip club opened it was harder to get booked to work there. A lot of the girls were trying to get in there. This caused the club to be very selective with the dancers, but then the hype would die down and they wouldn't be as picky.

Some of the men were the ultimate perverts. At times you could be doing your set and you could spot that one guy who was trying to be discreet while moving around in his seat. You knew he was helping himself sexually. The bouncer would throw him out if he was caught in the act. You learned to ignore this kind of thing while in the champagne room of course, because you wanted to make your money.

The male strip club where I used to work was having an event. It was their one year anniversary. It was an all white affair. I was excited to go. I knew it would be a fun evening out. I was picked up at home by a group of girls that I had met while working there. Everyone was dressed in white. It was a night of entertainment by the male dancers plus dancing on the dance floor. We were drinking a lot. I was quickly getting drunk.

I came across Fabian in the crowd. We spoke briefly and I became agitated with him about the fact that he hadn't called me. By that time I was being a bad drunk. I started to argue with him, and he said I was drunk and that he would be at a baseball game the next day, and that I should meet him there. He disappeared and I didn't see him for the rest of the night. My night didn't end on a good note. Of course the next day I was extremely hung over. I had some flashbacks of how I had acted during the night, and was disappointed at my behaviour. While working at one of Fabian's clubs I ran into him again. He asked why I hadn't shown up at the baseball game. I told him I hadn't remembered that I was to meet him at any baseball game. We spoke briefly, and after our conversation I decided that being friends with Fabian, and nothing more, was the best thing to do. I was embarrassed at my drunken state at the party. I was out of control and acted like a desperate woman. I didn't want to act like that again. I had seen too many women act that way, and I always thought they came across as desperate and needy. That wasn't me. I didn't want any drama.

We are Family

Not too long after all this; Jake came back to Ottawa for good. It was different having him back in my life on a regular basis. With him home, it allowed me more freedom to work more often.

At times I went out of town to work. The pay was higher, which allowed me to spend more time at home when I returned. It was hard to leave, and even harder when I returned. Cassie started to give me the cold shoulder as her way to punish me for leaving. Everything was Dad. She kept me at arms length, but as the days went on she warmed up to me again.

Travelling Again

I went to work in a club located in Fort Erie. The best thing about working at this club was its location. It was at the U.S. and Canadian border, so most of the money we made from table dancing was American currency.

That week, both customers and dancers kept commenting that I resembled Janet Jackson. I didn't see any similarities and I thought their comments were inaccurate. Her music was very popular at the time. I thought she was an excellent dancer and I loved her songs, which were included in some of my sets.

They also thought the bartender resembled the black guy from Miami Vice, which I had to agree with. They also commented that they thought we should get together, which of course never happened. Later, when Janet Jackson's movie Poetic Justice came out she wore long braids. It was a popular style, which became a trademark hairstyle for me. I got even more remarks about our resemblance than before.

Another place I enjoyed working was the Army base in Petawawa. This club was full of army guys. A lot of the Canadian Forces lived there. They were a fun group to be around. At first, I felt intimidated by their uniforms, but they made me feel at ease right away. One thing I noticed about them, as rowdy as they were, they were very polite. I had a lot of marriage proposals that week.

Jake, Cassie and I moved to a nicer apartment. It was located in a better neighbourhood and we were on the twelfth floor in a well-kept building. I kept working, but once again, I was getting tired of the men, the drinking and drugs. It started to take a toll on me. I realized this more so, when I ended up working with a dancer who was from out of town. Kate and her boyfriend were from the U.S. He was a football player, and a really big guy. Their accents were very Southern, which I liked.

Experiencing Freebasing

One day after our shift, Kate and her boyfriend gave me a ride home, and I invited them up to our apartment to meet Jake. We had a couple of drinks and they asked us if we were into doing coke or freebasing. I had no idea what freebasing was, but my drug of choice was cocaine. I enjoyed the buzz

I got from coke, so I was up for trying it. Freebasing, as I observed, was when you placed an amount of cocaine into a spoon, then added heat by placing a lighter underneath it. The fumes from it was collected into a bottle, which then we would take a hit off the bottle (inhale the fumes). Right away there was a rush of an intense feeling of pleasure; the high itself lasted about half an hour. We also mixed the cocaine with hash by rolling them both together into a joint; we were up for quite sometime. Later, as morning was approaching, they left. I hated the next day after getting high. I was very irritated and tired. I just wanted to stay in a quiet dark room and sleep, but when Cassie was with us, we had to suck it up and deal with it. Jake always bounced back faster than I did maybe because he was six-two and weighed almost two hundred pounds.

It was after a night like that that I knew I needed to change my lifestyle. I was drinking, and doing a lot more drugs than usual. I spoke with Jake about needing a change, and we went through all my options. One of my options was enrolling in cosmetology school; I enjoyed working with cosmetics.

I needed to occupy myself with something that was normal.

The Academy

I applied to Versailles Academy, and was accepted. It was a well known academy. I got a grant from the government to attend. The program wasn't quite a year, but at the end of the semester you received a certificate. I was very excited about the turn of events in my life. It had been a long time since I had studied anything.

My first day was refreshing. I thought "This was what normal people do". The instructors looked beautiful with their perfect make-up and well groomed hair. They wore white coats that reminded me of a scientist or doctor. A tour of the academy along with the rules and expectations were given. We were also given a bag that contained a large black casing with many colours of eye shadows, blushes and lip-glosses. It seemed to have every-thing a woman needed. You had to purchase the skin care products separately.

There were twenty of us in the class. I recognized one of the students from a club. Later, after our sessions ended for the day, I went over and introduced myself. Her name was Sachi. She was pretty with Italian heritage. I asked her where she worked. She said at the moment she wasn't working, but had worked as a waitress in a strip club. I mentioned that I had seen her before during the changing over between our shifts. It was brief. Some clubs were busy like that.

We laughed at the odds of running into each other. We became friends, and helped each other out through the process of our career change. Sachi was dating one of the bouncers from that club. Occasionally, she cared for an older gentleman. She said their relationship wasn't sexual, but it was for companionship.

We put Cassie in a daycare that was close to the academy. Jake got a job as a taxi driver. This was helpful with our new schedule. He worked through the nights. In the morning he arrived with breakfast, and dropped me off at school and Cassie at daycare.

Sometimes after our classes, I went home with Sachi to her chic apartment. It wasn't far from the school. Some days I brought Cassie along. When we were ready to go home, Jake would come to pick us up. I enjoyed spending time with Sachi. We could talk and laugh about our experiences in the clubs.

I appreciated everything the academy had to offer. I learned a lot of techniques about skin care and applying cosmetics. I also discovered a few things about myself. I learned that I had a heart-shape face, and a classic style. Dressing up each day, putting on my best outfits, and make-up, well groomed hair and well-done manicure hands, made me feel like a lady. It was fun working on my other classmates and bringing in models to display what we had learned from each session. I didn't like doing pedicures, especially when we had to practice on clients from outside the academy. Some feet were not pleasant to look at, or to even handle with gloves. I knew pedicures were not in my future plans.

At the end of our intense course it was time to graduate. I was sad and excited at the same time. I looked forward to my future, in hopes of a job in my field.

I got connected to a program for women only. It was to help me re-enter the retail workforce. The program also helped with my résumé writing, and taught me how to conduct myself in an interview. I found the group meetings uncomfortable. We had to share our feelings, weaknesses, and strengths. These were questions I had never thought about before. I found them difficult to answer. I remember referring to myself, as "Elegant Elaine". Maybe that's what I aspired to be.

At the end of the program we were given a list of companies, which supported the program. From this list we had to choose the companies we were interested in doing a placement with. Our fine-tuned resumes were sent to the companies in hopes of an interview. If they called, the possibility of being hired was in your favour.

Sachi and I tried to stay in touch, but our different schedules made it difficult to stay connected.

Hired

I got a job at Bayswater. It was one of the companies from my list. This department store was expensive with a large cosmetics and fragrance section. The best part about my placement was its location. It was at the shopping centre that was close to my parent's home, which came in handy.

My placement at the store was a good experience. I enjoyed working in a vibrant and glamorous environment. One of my co-workers and I had been to elementary and high school together. I was relieved, because she didn't probe me about leaving high school. Working in that atmosphere was extremely positive.

The day arrived to find out whether or not I would be kept on as an employee. The supervisor was generous in her evaluation of me and had decided to hire me. It was a part-time position, but I was elated. Finally, I had a regular job doing something I enjoyed! With my new job I felt I was fitting into the workforce like everyone else.

It was while working at this store I met Ellen. She was in her mid-forties, beautiful, with blond hair and piercing blue eyes. She had an accent, as she was from Ireland. We became friends. She had been in the cosmetics business for a while, and offered to help me whenever I needed it.

A Better Offer

I had been working at Bayswater for six-months, when Ellen announced she was leaving. She had received an offer for a management position at Bensons. It was a new department store downtown. Best of all, she wanted me to join her! She offered me a full-time position in the cosmetics and fragrance department that she was going to manage.

I was elated and thanked her for the offer, but told her I needed to speak with Jake first. After speaking with Jake, we both decided it was a good opportunity, especially working full-time. By now we had moved into a house. Our rent was based on our income. Jake had left the taxi business, and was working as a sales representative at a car dealership. He worked long hours and it was difficult at times, but it was a different job, and more stable hours.

I contacted Ellen immediately to accept the position. We both left Bayswater to the new store very excited.

The store was located in the largest mall downtown. This was where all the action was. It was a bit intimidating at first working downtown. I had to get use to taking the bus. Jake usually drove me everywhere. I saw a lot of people hustling and bustling about. It was a complete different vibe, than what I was familiar with. It was a new world. I thought "This is what normal people do with their lives". At times I felt out of place, but it was an improvement compared to the club life.

Things changed drastically for me, but were good changes. At the age of twenty-five, I thought, "This is the best time in my life!" I was in a good job as a cosmetician, which I enjoyed, a mother to the sweetest little girl, and in a common-law relationship. We lived in a nice home, and my parents had purchased a home ten minutes away from us.

Having Ellen as my manager was the best. We enjoyed working together. She favoured me over the other co-workers by giving me the best shifts, and time off. Sometimes we took our lunch breaks together, during which, we had a couple of glasses of wine. After a while I learned that Ellen was a drinker. There were times when she showed up for work and I was sure she was tipsy. I could smell alcohol on her breath. At first I thought it was mouthwash, but then I realized it was more than that. Ellen was a smoker too, so the smell of the nicotine helped camouflage the smell of the booze. She would stumble here and there, but not falling down drunk. She was still able to function. She was happy and funnier when she had been drinking and I found out later that her drink of choice was vodka. My experience from working in the clubs was that vodka was a drink that didn't have a strong scent. I never mentioned what I suspected to Ellen. I figured she was handling it, and in full control.

One day while on my lunch break, I went to Meyers. This was another major department store also located in the mall. A beautiful black lady was behind the counter of a product line for darker skin tones. We had a good conversation. I told her where I worked, and after our conversation she asked if

I wanted to work at her make-up counter for a few extra hours. She said it was very busy during promotional times like Christmas. I said, "Yes" as it was extra money.

Everything was going great! Jake had changed jobs, and was working at the post office plant on the night shift. The new job enabled him to be home when Cassie came from school. I was with her during the evenings into the night. During this time I continued to drink and get high, but not as much as before.

The Affair, the Married Man

A few weeks after I started working at Bensons, Robert walked into my life. I noticed Robert one day while he was walking through the store. I found out he was one of the store managers. There were five managers, who worked in rotation at the branches around Ottawa. Robert started visiting our department frequently. At first he made small talk with everyone, but I noticed that his attention had turned to me. I didn't read much into it until one day when Ellen had made a comment. She believed he was coming to the department specifically to see me. I told her that things were going good in my life, and that I was not interested in getting involved with anyone-well so I thought.

Robert was persistent and made it known that he was interested. He wasn't discreet. Ellen said he was too obvious, and that my co-workers might figure it out. Robert was in his late thirties, handsome and usually wearing a suit. He was always well groomed. And, judging by the ring on his finger, he was also married. In our conversations I mentioned that I was in a common-law relationship, and a mother, but Robert still pursued with interest.

I started looking forward to Robert's visits. Whenever I heard his name being paged over the intercom, I knew he was in the store, and a feeling of excitement stirred inside me. I would check myself in the mirror to make sure I looked ok, just in case Robert came by my department, which he ultimately did, and we would flirt with each other.

After months of flirting, Robert suggested we get together. At first the thought scared me, but was exciting. I told Ellen about Robert's invitation, and how I felt. Considering his position at the store, she was surprised he had asked me out. She thought there was no harm in going out with him, given that we were attracted to each other. She also said a lot of married men had affairs. I thought about what I should do. I decided to go.

Robert and I made plans on a night I knew Jake wasn't working. This meant I didn't have to rush home to relieve him from taking care of Cassie, so he could sleep before work.

After my shift, I met Robert outside the mall at the designated location. There I was sitting in his car. I hadn't a clue where we were going. I became extremely nervous. Robert seemed to sense my nervousness and admitted that he was nervous too. We reached our destination a short time later and I recognized where we were as we approached the building. It was a hotel near the mall. Robert drove through the hotel's underground garage and as he led the way we had pointless nervous conversations.

The hotel was very fancy, and I was sure it was very expensive. I noticed as we entered the room that it had a kitchenette, and a sitting area. Robert told me the room was being rented by a friend, who was new in town. His friend was Bensons' new Regional Manager. He was staying at the hotel until he found a house for him and his family. After hearing this I had a lot of questions. "Was this something Robert had done before?" "Did his friend know who I was?" Robert's answers to all my questions were "No". He was persuasive, and I believed him.

He offered me a drink, and I agreed to some white wine. He poured for both of us. We sat together on the couch. We started talking about Bensons' stores and life in general. While in the process of our conversation my thoughts drifted to the fact that I wouldn't see Cassie before bed. I spoke with her earlier when I phoned home. It was a mistake to have met with Robert. I thought "What am I doing here?" "Why did I agree to come?" I had lied to Jake about where I was going. I told him after work I was going out with Ellen for drinks. I felt torn between wanting to be there, and wanting to go home.

I was startled out of my thoughts when Robert kissed me. I asked him to wait and he asked what was wrong. I told him how I felt about being there, and the fact that we were both in relationships. He said it was ok, and that he understood. So, we sat in silence, and then Robert offered to take me home if I wanted to leave. I was attracted to Robert, and knew I wasn't ready to go home yet. I said I was fine and then he leaned over and kissed me again, but this time I returned his kiss. We ended up crossing the boundaries that two people shouldn't cross while in a committed relationship. As we were getting dressed I felt ashamed and guilty.

Robert drove me home. The ride was quiet. I got out of the car on the street before my street. We had a quick kiss good night.

Jake was still up when I got home. He wanted to know how my night went with Ellen. I told him it was nice and that we had had a good time. I didn't want to go into any details, so I quickly changed the subject to Cassie. I said I was tired and heading up to bed. I went to check on Cassie and felt a wave of guilt after seeing her. I took a shower and went straight to bed. I was tired from my long day, but my thoughts were replaying the night's event, which left me feeling terrible about myself.

I thought because of how I felt after the first time there wouldn't be a second, but there was. Robert came to see me a few days later. We spoke briefly. My responses were quick and short. Before he left he gave me a number to contact him anytime.

The next day I called. I led the conversation in the direction of our relationships. Robert said he loved his wife, but was attracted to me. He wanted to spend time with me. I told him I was attracted to him too, but I didn't like the way I felt. We agree to meet again and once again I used Ellen as an excuse to be away from home.

Robert picked me up after my shift, and we headed to our destination. Later as we drove up in front of the house he told me that it was his house. I was shocked, and taken off guard with this information. He said his wife was out of town for a couple of days. I became upset that he had brought me there. What was he thinking? He reassured me that everything was fine, and that his wife was hours away in another city.

We proceeded to go inside. As he led the way I felt very uneasy being at his home. Once inside the uneasiness grew when I saw all the photos of him and his wife. I tried not to focus or think about where I was. I didn't want to ruin another night together. He handed me a glass of wine, and after a couple of glasses I felt more relaxed. We went downstairs to his recreational room where we spent the evening.

This became a regular occurrence when his wife was out of town. I was officially having an affair with a married man. This relationship went on for a year and a half. I was living two completely different lives. I was in a common-law relationship and a mother in one, which was like being married without the legality. And in the other, I was the girlfriend, mistress of a married man. My relationship with Robert was solely based on physical attraction. I felt I had a family life with Jake. In my mind, this was how I justified my actions.

An Eye Opener

At times things got difficult to handle. Although I hated lying with secret phone calls, and meetings, we continued with the relationship. One night, it was as if I had awakened out of a dream. That was the day I saw Robert's wife for the first time in person. It was at the company's annual Christmas party. I was surprised at my willingness in wanting to go. I didn't usually go to those types of events. All employees were encouraged to attend with anticipation that the company would be putting on a special event. Most employees I knew were going. So, I told Jake about the party, and that it sounded like a fun night. We decided to go.

When we arrived at the party a lot of people were already there. We got our seats, and I scanned the room to locate Robert. Finally, my eyes landed on him, and his wife, she was pregnant. I thought she looked prettier in person with her blonde hair all done up elegantly.

The night was fun with a lot of laughter. It was murder mystery night. During the night, Robert and my paths never crossed. I did notice when he and his wife got up and made their way to the dance floor. That was the moment that it hit me, that I had to stop seeing Robert. I knew his wife was pregnant, because he told me when they found out. Therefore seeing his wife pregnant shouldn't have affected me, but it did! We used to talk about what he was experiencing while she was pregnant. We spoke about his expectations and how he was looking forward to becoming a father. Seeing them there together made it all seem real.

Then I started thinking about Jake and how hurt he would be if he knew about Robert and me. The feelings of guilt were stirring. It was as if something suddenly jolted me awake, and there was a spotlight on Robert and his wife. Both of us were in serious relationships. We should not have been seeing each other. I remember watching them dance, and then leave the party shortly afterward.

The following week Robert came by the department as usual. He wanted to know if I had enjoyed the party. I told him that Jake and I had had a good time, and I mentioned how I felt seeing his pregnant wife. She was almost due to give birth and he was very excited about the coming birth of the baby, and the fact that it was a boy. I was excited for him too, and I knew this relationship had to come to an end.

After that day we mostly spoke on the phone. Robert joined a baseball team, and sometimes had games close to my house. One night, he wanted to meet up after his game. I had been drinking before I saw him, and was drunk. When we met I blurted out how I felt about our relationship, and the fact that he and his wife were having a child. I told him that we shouldn't be seeing each other anymore. We went back and forth in our discussion. The conversation was upsetting. Robert said he understood how I felt, but thought things were good the way they were, and I shouldn't be so concerned. I disagreed. He didn't like the fact that I was drunk and drove me home. I waited for a week before calling him after that unpleasant incident. Our conversation was casual, but after his son was born I stopped calling.

I was sure at some point Jake had suspected something was going on, but he never brought it up.

That experience left me in a bad state. I felt empty. The drinking, and getting high increased again. I was struggling being at work and hated being there. I told Ellen I wanted to work part-time hours only and she agreed. Being at work reminded me too much of Robert and our relationship. Even though he no longer came to see me, I knew when he was in the store. I no longer wanted to work there and told Jake that there were a lot of changes in management, and I didn't like working there anymore. I wanted to leave and Jake was supportive of my decision.

Because our rent was based on our income, I knew I could take some time before moving on to my next job.

I was content with being at home. I was taking care of my family full-time. I enjoyed cooking, cleaning and all the things that went with being a full time homemaker. Unfortunately, that didn't last long. I became bored with my new routine within weeks. I slipped into the habit of filling my days with watching movies, and getting high during the hours Cassie was at school. Later, when she was in bed, I relaxed with a few drinks.

After I left the store, Ellen and I stayed in touch. One day, she called with bad news. Ellen had had breast cancer before, but it had been in remission, but it had returned. I went to visit her at home.

Over the years I had met her husband and teenage daughters. They were a nice family. I would like to say that I was there for Ellen during this time, but I wasn't. I was drowning in self-pity on a downward spiral of depression. I stayed home most of the time. I didn't have a social life, and I didn't care for anyone outside my home to know the state that I was in, not even my family. Jake kept active with his sports, which caused problems in our relationship. I wanted him to stay home with me. So he would go out to his games and rushed back home afterward, but I still wasn't happy. I tried going to some of his games, but I hated the aggressiveness.

While I was at home I became more aware of our next-door neighbour. She and her boyfriend lived together with their young daughters. I didn't care for them, especially her. She didn't work and spent most of her time at home strung out. When I saw her kids they looked dirty, and unkempt. She often yelled at them and told them to go outside to play while she stayed inside getting high. There were people coming and going to their house con-stantly. It was a party house and their partying was affecting us. The noise that came through our thin walls was disruptive. We would ask them to keep it down, but our requests weren't received nicely. We decided it was best to move to another area. Jake called the rental company to see if we could move. It wasn't easy moving within the rental units. The waiting list was very long. Getting a transfer would take a long time. I hated where I lived.

Tested For AIDS

To make matters worse I received a letter stating that I needed to get tested for AIDS, because of the blood transfusion I had received after giving birth to Cassie. This was at the time when AIDS first came out and people were dying soon after being infected. Around that time Jake kept getting sick. I mentioned the letter I had received to Jake, during that conversation he finally spoke about my lack of commitment to our relationship. He was very upset and agreed that it was a good idea for me to get tested.

The day I went to get tested was one of the scariest days in my life. While waiting for the results I took a hard look at my life. I regretted some of the choices I had made. Thank God all my tests came back negative.

A State of Depression

I felt like I was drowning in my feelings about my life. It wasn't the way I wanted it. I sank deeper into a state of depression. I wasn't content unless I was drinking or getting high. Jake suggested that I should see a counsellor. He thought I needed a professional to help me deal with my emotions. I agreed and chose a counsellor out of the phone book.

I had never gone to see a counsellor before. I wasn't sure I wanted to open up myself to anyone, especially a stranger, but I went. When I walked into her office, right away I felt I had made a mistake. We spoke about things that were concerning me, but not in great detail. I didn't want her to know too much about me. I focused our conversation on my neighbours, and how I felt unhappy and stressed out living beside them. At the end of our meeting I left feeling the same way I came.

I went to see my family doctor, and revealed more of my feelings of depression. She gave me a prescription for anti-depressant, and said they would help with my anxiety and stress. At first, I didn't mind taking the pills. They made me feel numb; made my mind shut down, like it was moving in slow motion. I couldn't function. My days were spent sleeping, and when I was awake it was as though I couldn't think. My head felt heavy. My shoulders felt as though they were fighting hard to keep my head up. I wasn't myself. After awhile I stopped taking the pills. I wasn't taking care of my family the way I wanted. I did however acquire a letter from my doctor to give to the rental company. The letter stated that I was suffering from anxiety and depression, which were brought on by our neighbours, and in order for me to get well I needed a new environment. We brought the letter to our rental company, and they agreed to allow us to choose another location.

We decided to take the first house we viewed. It was five minutes from our old house, and much nicer. We were closer to the street away from most of the other houses, which was nice. We were ecstatic with this new location. It was perfect for us. It was in walking distance from Cassie's school. I thought this was going to be the happiest we had ever been. But I would be proven wrong. I was on my way to hitting bottom.

CHAPTER SEVEN

Hitting Bottom

Moving into our new house, into a new location, was what I needed. It was a fresh start. I enjoyed being home, walking Cassie to school and picking her up. I spent time doing things that pleased me. I felt safer at home than being out in the world doing what others considered normal. I felt the world wasn't my world and had no place for me. I couldn't seem to function in it. I thought the best place for me would be at home taking care of my family.

A few years went by with me at home. Jake continued working at the post office. We were happy as a family. We even had a dog. We got him for Cassie who was now seven. He completed our little family.

One day, while out and about I ran into Teresa. She was a dancer I knew from before I had quit. She was from Puerto Rico. She was older than me, and had no tolerance for nonsense. She reminded me of myself. We had worked together on many occasions and got to know each other. We discovered through our conversations that we knew some of the same people, and her boyfriend was the younger brother of a guy from my high school. This was surprising. I considered her a dancer friend.

It was good seeing her again. She was still dancing. I was invited to her apartment and I went. We had fun catching up. Teresa surprised me with the news that she was pregnant. I was elated for her. I knew she would make a good mother. Teresa was responsible, a go getter, and always seemed in control. She confided in me that her relationship with her boyfriend was rocky. He had not been as committed to the relationship. He was a lot younger than her.

Hanging out with Teresa brought me back into the night life. One day, Jake came home with a surprise of sexy lingerie sets and white wine. I was happy for my surprise. We were settling in for a romantic night home. The phone rang and it was Teresa calling to invite me to go along with her to a club to freelance. Right away I was jolted with fear. I had not danced for a few years. Even though I had not gained a lot of weight, I didn't think I was close to the shape I was in when I left dancing, and I didn't know if Jake would agree for me to go. I wasn't sure I wanted to go back, but there had been times throughout the years that I did miss the club scene.

I told Teresa I had to speak to Jake and call her back. I spoke to Jake. He gave me the go-ahead if that was what I wanted to do. I felt his disappointment that I was leaving at that moment. He tried not to show it. I called Teresa to let her know I would go. I thought Jake showing up with lingerie and wine was a sign I was meant to go. I started getting ready. I kept drinking my wine extremely grateful I had it. I was full with fear and excitement at the same time.

Teresa picked me up and we headed to the club. It was a club I had worked at many times. Upon my arrival I saw some familiar customers in the crowd, which was surprising to me after all these years. But it did help to put me at ease. After getting changed and picking out our songs, we sat with a few of them going from table to table. I took the drinks that were offered to me. Teresa didn't drink any alcohol because of her condition. By the time it was my turn on stage I was no longer feeling fearful. I was drunk enough not to care. I did my set as best I could. I felt out of shape in the midst of it. I was glad to have gotten through my first set.

Back in that atmosphere, I felt at ease. I got caught up on some of the club activities from a few of the girls I knew. I did a number of table dancing, but discovered that I wasn't as comfortable doing them as I was being on stage. At the end of the night I was glad I went. It was like old times. I knew I wanted to return.

Doing What I Know Best

When I went home that night Jake was still up. I was drunk and tired, but excited to tell him about my night. I told him I wanted to return to dancing. That I missed the atmosphere and the money I made. I called the agency the next day and got booked at the club I went with Teresa. Since they knew who I was there was no problem booking me there. This decision to return to dancing would bring about many changes in my life.

I tried getting my scheduling for the day shifts, so that I could be home in the evenings before Cassie's bedtime. Working the evening shift was hard. It meant I saw Cassie in the mornings before school, and later at night when I checked on her after I came home. Sometimes, Jake brought me to work and I got a driver to return home. When he did pick me up unfortunately he had to bring Cassie along. All she knew was that mom was at work.

Returning to dancing was somewhat hard physically. It took time getting used to the extent of dancing that was required. I had to get used to table dancing all over again. I often started my shift with a couple of glasses of wine. This routine was helpful to get me into the swing of things.

I had a different outlook this time around as a dancer. Maybe it was because I was more mature than before. I treated it as a regular job. My focus was making money for my family. It wasn't about making money to buy things I wanted, but what my family needed, which added pressure on me to make a certain amount of cash each day.

With the customers, I acted extra friendly and became very flirtatious. I drank with them, which I didn't do much of in the previous years. I also got high with the girls I worked with. By the end of the night, I went home and passed out. On weekends I was extremely tired from my week, and I didn't want to do much of anything except sleep.

Out of Control

My routine however was affecting my relationship. When I was at home I was irritated. I felt more content at the club while drinking and getting high.

By now, Teresa had stopped dancing, but we kept in contact with each other. After her baby was born I went to visit. She was doing well, and the baby's father was still in the picture, but they were not together anymore. We got caught up, and I found out that she had plans to start her own escort business. We lost touch eventually. I don't know what happened to Teresa. Years later, her teenage daughter became a well known singer until this day.

As time went by I was developing a tolerance for drugs and alcohol. I started to do higher dosages of coke and smoking up on a regular basis. Getting high and drinking became normal to me. It was my reality. It was getting out of hand. It wasn't only when I was working, it was all the time.

I remember on one Canada Day; Jake and I were invited to a pool party. We took Cassie with us, with plans to see the fireworks later that night. It was a beautiful day. We arrived at the house early in the afternoon. When we got there the party was active with a lot of people intoxicated and high. We joined in the celebration. The day seemed to breeze by. The next thing I remember was Jake putting me into bed. I had blacked out. I was well intoxicated. I asked what about the fireworks and passed out. I had no idea what had occurred during most of the day. I felt horrible the following day from my hang over. I was also upset that I had missed the fireworks with my family. I was concern how my behaviour was during the day. What effect did it have on Cassie? Jake reassured me that everything was fine, and he had told Cassie that I was feeling sick and needed to go home to bed.

After my nights of drinking I did what people said to do. I got up and had another drink. I preferred a cold beer with clamato juice. It always mellowed me out. If I didn't take a drink I had the worst headache along with the shakes. I was irritated, and not the best person to be around. I had to push to function the next day because of Cassie.

On another occasion I was at work, and I drank until I blacked out. I was told later that a dancer had forgotten something in the changing room, and went back to retrieve it, and found me passed out on the floor. They had one of the regular customers drive me home. I found out the next day that he was very upset, because I threw up in his fancy sports car. Hearing this scared me. I thought this man could've done anything to me and I wouldn't have remembered.

My habit became more intense. I was always seeking out my next high. During this time I learned how to hide any signs of being high around my family. One day, while at my parent's home and having a drink with Daddy, and family friends he made the comment about me drinking like a man. It was the first time anyone had made any reference about my drinking. I am not sure why he made that statement but it stuck with me.

As my dependence increased, my relationship was decreasing. I felt as though, I was no longer able to continue in the relationship. I knew Jake wasn't happy with me. I wasn't satisfied being in the relationship. For the longest time I felt that there was something missing. I didn't know what it was. I kept hoping that I would figure it out, and things would change. With each passing day, I was getting worst and even at times becoming violent. I suggested to Jake maybe we should try and have another baby. This was going to be hard to accomplish since I had become distant from him. I felt torn in wanting to have my family life, but yet wanting to be free from the relationship. I was struggling.

Jake walked out of the house one day after we had a major fight. A few days later we spoke, and we made up. By the end of the week he returned home. I felt dreadful for him, Cassie and even myself when he was gone. I wanted him to be happy, but deep down I knew I wasn't the right person to accomplish this. I felt all through our relationship that I was the one who was the taker and not the giver. Jake took care of me most of the time. I had grown very dependent on him. I thought he was putting up with too much from me. He was more committed to our relationship than I was.

Trying to keep my family intact and satisfying myself became difficult. I was divided between two worlds again. I was trying to be a wife, a mother, and on the other hand a dancer. I thought being in a relationship, and having a family wouldn't have an effect on me going back to dancing, but it did. I constantly felt guilty being away from home. That I wasn't spending enough time there. When at work it seemed as if I was at one big party.

I became an expert in hiding the fact that I was high or drunk. I made sure I had Visine for my red eyes, and mouthwash or mints for my breath. They were a necessity to disguise the signs. I didn't consider myself to be a falling over drunk. Being under the influence did give me boldness. I had an "I don't care!" attitude most of the time. I found this liberating. Since my teenage years I cared too much about what others thoughts and opinions were of me.

My mood swings were mounting. One night, the DJ decided to give one of my songs to be used by another dancer without my permission. He thought I wouldn't use it during that shift. I freaked out! I became enraged. I started throwing chairs around. A couple of the girls managed to calm me down.

I became lenient when I was intoxicated and table dancing. I found myself not caring when the customers got too close or pretended it was an "accident" they had touched me. In the previous years, I would've gotten off the stool and demanded they pay me or walked away. It became difficult to look at myself in the mirror after awhile. I kept the lights off especially while I was in the bathroom. I didn't like the person I was changing into.

My relationship with Jake became increasingly difficult. I wanted out. I was torn between wanting him to stay around for Cassie's sake and my desire to end the relationship. My attitude wasn't attractive.

It didn't take much to set me off. I was restless when I wasn't working, and when I was working I wanted to be home. One day while Jake was sleeping before his shift I went and woke him up arguing about something irrelevant. He was infuriated; that I woke him up. We argued loudly. I hit him and ran into the bathroom. He started pounding on the door. I wouldn't open the door. He knocked the door off its hinges and grabbed me. I started hitting him while he was shaking me. This was a good thing for me, because one day when I was having one of my rages and I hit him, which was a common thing. He actually hit me back. When it happened it was shocking and painful. Jake had never hit me before no matter what I did. At this moment it was as if all our pent up frustration was being released. I was crying hard, and kept apologizing, but he was angry. He walked away and went downstairs. I followed after him full of regret for waking him up.

The Break Up

After we had both calmed down we started to talk. Our conversation was focused on my unhappiness throughout the years. We talked for a long time. I think at that moment we both knew our relationship had to come to an end. Jake was going to move out. He got some of his possessions and left. I didn't know where he was going, but I knew he had friends he could stay with.

The hardest thing about our decision to separate was having Cassie go through the experience of not having her parents living together. We tried to ease her into the change the best way we could. I continued to work. When I did, Jake came to stay with Cassie, which we had agreed upon. We thought this approach would allow them more time together.

Gradually Jake took items from the house he felt belonged to him. I wasn't going to argue about anything he wanted. I felt completely responsible that he was leaving. It was my fault our family was breaking up, and that he would have less time with his daughter.

Even though I was unhappy about the break up of our family, I felt it was the right thing to do. I felt free from all the guilt I had been carrying around. I was no longer living a lie, and being a hindrance to Jake finding real happiness. I thought with the relationship now terminated he might find someone who would love him the way he deserved.

Soon after our break up, I met Dave in one of the clubs. He was a lot older than I was, divorced, intellectual, and extremely calm. He was into Buddhism. He became one of my regular customers.

Dave came by the club after he finished work. He would stop by on his way home. We had a lot of conversations about a variety of topics. I thought he was interesting the more I spent time with him. In one of our conversations the manner in which he spoke to me caused me to think about my life. One night, he asked if I would join him for dinner at his home. I said "Yes." The next day, Jake came by the house to stay with Cassie. I told him I would be late coming back that night.

Dave showed up towards the end of my shift. He took me to his home. I knew he had a good paying job, so I wasn't surprised at the elaborate house I saw. He offered me a glass of wine after we had settled in his kitchen. He started to cook, and I decided to ask him questions on the subject of his family and his divorce. He had been divorced for a few years. He told me it didn't end well. His ex-wife had gotten full custody of their children, and he saw them every other weekend. His wife had filed for the divorce. I got the impression he didn't see it coming and it wasn't something he wanted. He was having a hard time handling the separation of his family. I felt sorry for him.

We had supper and afterwards we sat talking some more with the focus on my life and why I was dancing. He was the first customer that had shown genuine interest in what was going on in my life. Maybe that's why I agreed to go to his home. The night ended with us in bed. And so began my relationship with Dave. At times he would pick me up after work and I would go directly to his home for a few hours before heading home, so that Jake could leave for work. This arrangement after a while became uncomfortable. I never forgot the moment we pulled up to my house one night in the process of Dave dropping me off, and Jake happened to be at the sink in the kitchen. The sink was located below the window that looked outside to the cul-de

-sac of my house. I knew he was aware that I was being dropped off by a guy I had been out with, and it didn't feel right. It wasn't a good idea. The arrangement had to be changed.

Now, a single mother by choice, I switched clubs. I started working at a club that was closer to home. I was able to work as a house girl doing the day shift. This club was more convenient because of its location. It enabled me to be home shortly after Cassie returned from school. I didn't continue to see Dave after switching clubs, because I wanted to focus on being a mother.

Sometimes I took weeks off from work to spend quality time with Cassie. Even though being at home with Cassie was enjoyable the adjustment of being a single mother, and a woman on my own was very difficult. I was lonely. I continued to drink. I made sure I always had something in the house to drink. My drugs came from the clubs, so when I wasn't working I had no access to drugs. There was a wine store within walking distance at the plaza, which was convenient since I wasn't driving. I had gotten my license and bought a Pontiac Trans Am, but was in the process of getting it on the road

Drinking became my best companion. I continue to drink enough during the days to get me through. After Cassie came home we had time together and when she went to bed I continued drinking.

The New Bouncer

I went back to work after a break, and discovered the club had hired a new bouncer. He was a handsome black man. His name was Wade. He was intimidating to look at, soft spoken, friendly and I thought very quiet. I also saw another side to him when someone got drunk and out of line. He knew how to get his point across. We said "Hello" to each other, but that was as far as our conversation went.

Lauren, (also a house girl) and I became close friends. In one of our conversations I discovered she was living on the same street as my parents. She lived with her boyfriend and her two kids. Lauren's boyfriend had formerly been one of her customers. Before meeting this guy, she was in an abusive relationship with the father of her kids. She was very happy in her new relationship, which was the opposite of what she had experienced in the past.

It was a familiar story for some of the girls. It was common to come across a dancer who was dating an individual they had met in the club, or they somehow became a part of your life. It could lead to marriage as it did for Lauren. One day, she came to work very excited with the news that her boyfriend had proposed. They were engaged. I was filled with joy for her. I thought marriage would lead her into having a normal life.

Sometimes, when visiting my parents I would drop by Lauren's house. They had a pool in their back yard, which the kids enjoyed. Spending time with her was a change for me. We didn't focus on life in the clubs, but on our families. I preferred being around people who knew how to separate the two.

On one of our shifts, Lauren brought up the discussion of Wade. She thought he was truly a nice guy and a big teddy bear, and suggested how nice it would be if I went out on a date with him. She thought we made an excellent couple, even though we had not gone out as yet.

For the next couple of days, Lauren made it her mission to bring both of us together. Well, her hard work paid off. One day, after my shift Wade asked me out on a date. As lonely as I had been feeling, I wasn't sure I was up to dating again, but said "Yes."

First Date

Wade took my address and picked me up at home Saturday night. Cassie was away at Jake's. He had his own apartment. She spent occasional weekends with him.

Going out with Wade was different. It felt as if it was my first date since Jake and I went out. I considered it an actual date. I was excited to be out with him. I had no idea where we were going. We ended up at a nice restaurant. In deep conversation we shared and exchanged some things about ourselves. I found out Wade was from Hamilton, Ontario. He was going to Carleton University in Ottawa; he used to play football in College. His goal was to work with troubled youth, which I thought was inspiring. After our time at the restaurant, Wade suggested taking me to a club in Hull.

He mentioned the name of the club, I had no idea where it was, but it was a favourite of his. I agreed. We headed to Hull.

It was Saturday night, which meant it was very busy on the strip. We finally found parking in one of the lots, and headed to the club. As we got closer to the club, I didn't recognize it, or knew it existed. I thought it was funny for all the times I had been to Hull I never went to many dance clubs. I always ended up in strip clubs.

I was impressed with the way Wade handled himself amongst the crowd. Maybe it was his intimidating appearance at first glance. He held my hand tight while he made his way through the crowd making sure not to let go of my hand. We were able to make our way to the bar and got our drinks. I watched how Wade interacted with those around us. I could tell he was a people person. He connected with people instantly.

Wade loved music especially hip hop. This club was playing hip hop and jumping. It was packed with people.

We were having a fun time dancing. We stayed until closing, and headed back to the parking lot to leave. I went to put on my coat, which was left in the car. I didn't want to check it at the door. But my coat was nowhere to be found. Wade said "I think I know what happened to your coat", and he had me sit in the car, saying he would be right back. I had no idea what was going on, or where he was going. In a short period of time I saw him coming towards me with my coat in his hand. I asked where he got it from; he responded from his ex-girlfriend. He mentioned seeing her during the night, and put two and two together. She still had a key to his car. She thought it would be funny to take the coat. He said she had apologized for taking the coat, and didn't know the coat belonged to me. Wade was furious, and made sure she knew it. He confiscated the key back from her. I was disturbed, that she thought it was a funny thing to do. I thought "What did I get myself into with this guy?" Here we were on our first date and there was drama already created by an ex-girlfriend. I didn't find her actions humorous at all.

Wade wanted us to stop for something to eat. I declined. I wanted to go straight home. He explained he had known his ex-girlfriend from high school. They had been dating since College. The relationship fell apart over a period of time, but in the end they remained friendly. I said "I understood", but I still wanted to go home. I knew he was disappointed.

He pulled up to my house and apologized again. I voiced my regret our night ended the way it did. We had had a good time together. He hoped what took place wouldn't prevent me from seeing him again. I said I would see him at work and bid him good night.

I was glad to be home. As I lay in bed I reflected over my date with Wade. I had a good time. I liked him. I knew within myself I wanted to see him again.

On Monday I returned to work. Wade wasn't there as his shift started in the evening. I kept watching the door for when he would arrive. Finally, he entered. I waited for a while before going to say hello. He seemed happy to see me, and once again apologized for our night ending the way it did. He wanted to know if I had thought about giving him another opportunity to take me out again. I said I did, which made us chuckle. From that day, Wade became a friend, and we started our relationship.

I was glad I didn't allow one moment to decide whether or not I would continue to see Wade. I would've missed out on knowing a genuinely nice guy. He was attentive especially when I was working. It was weird dating him and having him working there. It made me self conscious, even shy. Thankfully, we were only together on the same shift for a short period of time. My shift ended an hour after Wade arrived.

Wade added a lot of light to my life. He was encouraging and caring, and came with a lot of culture I felt I had been missing. He was up to date with current events. Because most of my time was spent in the clubs I realized I wasn't in tune with what was going on outside of that environment. The people I knew and hung out with were from the clubs. Our conversations were about the clubs, drugs or who had gotten arrested or getting out from jail.

Because I worked days, and Wade worked nights we saw each other on the weekends. After dating for a month we became intimate. I spent time at his apartment, which he shared with another guy from his home town.

I kept my dating life separate from my life with Cassie. I never allowed anyone I dated to come into my home or meet Cassie. I was okay with her having one man play an important part in her life, which was her dad. I kept in mind the experiences I had encountered with men and didn't trust them around my daughter. It would take a while before I would invite Wade to my house or to meet Cassie.

Vacation in Jamaica

Momma and Deirdre were making plans to go to Jamaica. They encouraged me to go along. It had been a long time since I visited back home. I decided to go and take Cassie with me. She had never been to Jamaica or anywhere outside of Canada. I thought it would be important for her to see where her mom came from and meet our family.

The time came for us to leave, which we counted down with great anticipation and excitement.

Jamaica was beautiful and as welcoming as I remembered. It was extremely hot. We had made arrangements to spend our first week at a resort. One of Momma's brothers was the owner. The second week we would head down to the country to see Aunt Pat.

We were like tourists hanging out at the resort. Because of the time of season, it wasn't as busy. Cassie had fun having the entire pool to herself most days, and spent a lot of time in it. It was a beautiful place with all its vibrant colours. There were peacocks walking around, which added to our experience and beauty of the place. A couple of Momma's brothers were there too. It was fun spending time with them. The meals were excellent. One day, along with a couple who was staying at the Villa, we all went on a boat ride to Dunn's River Falls. It is one of the favourite sites for tourists. On our boat ride we were served a tasty rum punch. Sailing on the water was peaceful and refreshing. We got to Dunn's River, it was beautiful. The water was powerful, and the force from it pushed hard against our bodies as we sat there taking in the experience. Our tour guides led us on a pathway over the falls. As we went up the falls, our feet came across groves in the rocks that seemed to be carved out to hold them.

The husband of the couple had to be rescued a few times. He was drunk. Most of the time one of my uncles had to retrieve him. He was having the time of his life; he wouldn't think so the next day when he would wake up with a hangover.

Now into our second week we headed to the country. Well, when we arrived I thought we should have visited there first, and ended our trip at the resort. It was the opposite of what we had experienced there. The insects were the worst. Everywhere you turned there were insects. Cassie was not impressed. She hated it. I felt bad for her. She hadn't experienced an assortment of insects like that before. When I was with Jake, we had bought a large size trailer, which was located on a camp ground outside of Ottawa. We would spend time there during the summer months. Our neighbour was a friend of Jake's, who he got drugs from, so my time there was getting high all day.

Cassie seemed to like it there except for getting stung by bees twice. But being here in the country was beyond what she had ever experienced at the campsite.

It was good seeing Aunt Pat and the rest of the family again after all those years. My Aunt Pat seemed smaller but strong. One day, I sat in the yard speaking to an elderly lady about life; it was a moment that brought me back to my childhood days. As I sat there I also reflected on my life in Canada. It didn't measure up to what I wanted. I didn't like what I saw.

Our trip to Jamaica was one that was overdue. I was glad I went, and that I brought Cassie. She has never forgotten our trip. She did have an enjoyable time in spite of the bugs. Unfortunately, a couple of weeks after leaving Jamaica I would lose a family member to death. Aunt Florence passed away. I had to return to Jamaica.

This time around Daddy, Deirdre and I headed to Jamaica. Cassie stayed with Jake. I was sad to be returning for this occasion. It wasn't expected.

We got through the grieving part of Aunt Florence passing with lots of stories of remembrance of her.

Old Relationships

The second part of our trip we spent catching up with people we knew from our neighbourhood. When I was growing up in Jamaica I had a childhood friend Lenny. He and I would always hang out. As young as we were it seemed as though we connected. We thought we would grow up and marry each other. On my first visit we didn't spend much time together. On my return we had more of an opportunity to hang out.

He picked me up one night from Aunt Pat's and took me to an outdoor party. At the party I was drinking, and feeling good in the warmth of the atmosphere of Jamaica. I missed Cassie, but was glad to have left behind all my problems and the cold winter of Canada.

Hours later, Lenny and I left the party. We headed back to his place, and spent time catching up and going down memory lane. He told me he had loved me from when we were young and had cried when I left. He said he still loved me. This was all news to me but was nice to hear.

I am not sure if it was the alcohol consumption, the reminiscing, and hearing him say he still loved me that found me once again being unfaithful. I would be intimate with him that night. We parted with me promising I would stay in contact. I would leave Jamaica a couple of days after.

Before I left Jamaica I purchased a bottle of Jamaica's popular white rum. This rum I grew up with. It had a very potent smell. Maybe it was because it was 63% high in alcohol. It didn't take much of it to get you drunk. When I was younger the slightest smell would make me feel like passing out. I could smell it in the rum punch at my parent's parties or their friends. It did give a nice taste I discovered later when I would sneak a taste or two. It was especially yummy in Momma's Christmas cakes, which is always popular with family and friends.

Returning home to Canada brought me back to reality. I was happy to be home to see Cassie and Wade. I thought about whether or not to admit my unfaithfulness to him. I decided against it. I couldn't bear the thought of hurting someone who had shown kindness and care to me once again.

Crashing

We continued to date. Wade surprised me one day and asked me if I would marry him? I was shocked and surprised! I thought it had been too short a period since we had been dating for him to decide he wanted to marry me. I told him he had to give me some time. I didn't think I was ready to be a wife. I suggested if we were together a year later, then I would marry him. He agreed.

Even though I was more content going out with Wade I still found myself drinking in large consumption. My favourite drink was mixing white rum with all kinds of fruit juices. Then I started to mix it with beer.

I was starting to feel pain inside my body as if my organs were hurting me. I pushed it aside. I thought I functioned better when I was drinking or high. I felt they filled the void I felt. They satisfied my inner need. When I wasn't drinking I was unhappy.

All sorts of thoughts ran through my mind. Drinking kept me going each day.

Night of Anguish

One night however, everything came crashing down. Cassie was away spending time with Jake. I had been drinking by myself, consuming large amounts of white rum and beer. I felt sick, nauseous. I ran to the bathroom and started throwing up. The room began to spin out of control. My head was throbbing loudly from throwing up so much. I felt as though my organs were going to come right out of my mouth. Every time I threw up it felt like my insides were coming out. I was in pain, and my body was hurting inside and out. There I was with my face hanging over the toilet bowl in a state that was familiar, but this time around it was so much more intense. I had gotten drunk and thrown up before but nothing like this. It was as if my organs had had enough of all the drugs and alcohol I had ever consumed and had decided they weren't going to take it any more. They were throwing it all back out. I panicked! I didn't know what to do.

I couldn't stop throwing up. I started to cry like a baby. I wanted it all to stop! I wanted the pain I was feeling all through my body, and the pounding of my head, which seem to increase in strength each time I threw up to stop! I did the only thing I could. I cried out to God. I found myself crying out to God "Please help me!" I said "If you help me, if you make this all stop I will never touch another drink or get high again!" "Clean me up!" "I want to change!" "Make it all stop!" All my years of getting high and drinking had finally caught up with me. I had now hit my bottom. It was while my head was hanging over the toilet bowl that I made the decision that I wanted to turn away from the life I was living. I wanted my life to change, to be better. I needed to change. I slipped to the floor, and there I lay. I passed out. I didn't know Jesus heard me.

CHAPTER EIGHT

Jesus Heard Me

*I love the Lord, because he hath heard my voice
and my supplications. Because he hath inclined
his ear unto me, therefore will I call upon him as
long as I live. (Psalms 116:1-2)*

At the time, I didn't speak to anyone about what I went through that night in the bathroom, not even to Wade. It wasn't until towards the end of the week that I realized I hadn't had a drink or had the desire to have a drink or get high. Days had passed by. On a regular day, I would've been looking forward to having a drink or smoking a joint.

Because Wade had no idea what had happened that night in the bathroom, he asked me to attend a club shortly after my incident. I didn't want to speak about it, so I agreed to go.

Club Shooting

We got to the club late and decided to sit at the bar. Our time was spent in conversation, and listening to the music. Having no desire to drink alcohol, my drinks all night were non-alcoholic. It was getting towards closing time and for the first time since Wade and I have been going out we decided to leave early, before the lights came on indicating the club was closing up. As we were leaving we passed a couple of guys who were coming in. This was not unusual, because there were always people popping into clubs at the last moment trying to get to the bar for that last drink. The next day, to our surprise we found out that a shooting had taken place after we left the club. The bartender had been shot. Fortunately, it wasn't fatal. That night was the last time I ever went into a night club.

Bible in the Club

The following week while I was at work, I went to the back to the dancers changing room. It was there as I entered the room I came across something I had not seen before. It was Lydia, one of the dancers reading her Bible. I commented on her reading her Bible. I said "Oh you are reading your Bible? I could never read my Bible". In my mind I was thinking how she could be reading her Bible in a strip club. I knew from the years I attended church as a little girl, that the state in which I was living my life was in rejection to God's principles. It was certainly not according to what I remember being taught in Sunday school. In fact, my life seemed to be in total disobedience. I had fallen far away from the right path.

Lydia, advised me to start by reading the book of John. I thanked her and said I would try. I had kept the small Bible I had received while becoming a citizen to Canada as a little girl. The next morning after searching, and finding my Bible I started to read John as Lydia had suggested. I found myself becoming emotional while reading through the chapters for some reason, and then I started to cry. I couldn't explain what I was experiencing or how I felt in the process while reading, but it was enough to make me go back over and over again. Reading through the book of John became part of my morning routine. I felt I had to read a part of it each day before heading out to work.

I found myself talking about God to my customers, and about my new experience. I tried to explain what was taking place within me, and my new outlook on life. I am not sure if I was able to articulate how I was feeling, but I knew what was taking place was good. I felt as though I was coming alive spiritually. I was seeing things differently. I started to look into different faiths, and requesting for brochures for more information, which I have never done before. In the end I came back to the Bible.

I decided to take my sister up on her offer to go to church with her the following Sunday. Deirdre would invite me to her church now and again, but I always had an excuse as to why I couldn't go. The truth was that I knew the night before I would be out drinking, and I certainly didn't want to go to church hung over. During our conversation on our way to church, Deirdre told me that she had run into Jessie downtown. She was working in office administration. Jessie was also pregnant and was a couple of weeks away from having her baby. Their conversation was brief. Deirdre thought Jessie looked the same, and happy. This was good news. I was happy for her, that her life had seemed to turn around.

Church Girl

I was nervous when the day arrived for me to go to church. It had been a very long time since I had been to church. I wasn't sure what I was going to encounter there. As I walked into the building, and heard the music playing, and saw the people all dressed up in their Sunday best, a flood of memory came back to me. It all seemed very familiar. It was what I remember as a young girl in Jamaica attending church with Aunt Pat. It felt good to be there. It was peaceful. I felt as if all was right with the world as I sat there listening to the songs, and hearing the preacher give his sermon. I honestly don't remember the topic on which he preached, because I was too caught up with just being there. Running through my mind were the thoughts that I wanted, and needed more of this exposure in my life.

After the service, I was introduced to one of the leaders in the church. Her name was sister Whalen. During our conversation I found out that she knew Daddy, and her husband had worked with him previously.

I thought sister Whalen was gentle and soft spoken. I liked her. We exchanged phone numbers. She told me that the women were having an upcoming prayer breakfast, and there would be a special speaker. I told her I would try to come.

I decided to go to the breakfast to see what it was all about. My decision to do so brought some excitement. I arrived half an hour after it had started. I was greeted at the door by some of the ladies who were there to welcome attendees and check their tickets. Since I wasn't sure I would go, I didn't purchase my ticket in advance, but you could get it at the door. After purchasing my ticket I walked towards the room where the breakfast was taking place. As I entered the room I was met with a striking scene. Most of the ladies were in full white from top to bottom, which was beautiful to see. Sister Whelan, saw me and waved at me to come over to where she was sitting. She expressed how happy she was to see me, and to join them. She introduced me to the ladies seated at the table. There were lots of conversations as we waited for our breakfast, which I found out would be served buffet style. Sitting there made me feel overwhelmed. I couldn't believe I was in that atmosphere amongst these ladies. Being in their midst and listening to their conversations about God was so inspiring. The breakfast session was filled with inspiring words from the speaker, and songs sang by a talented young lady. I left the breakfast uplifted and very encouraged.

A few weeks later, sister Whalen told me the church would be hosting a concert. She thought it would be enjoyable for me to attend, and so I went. I was pleasantly surprised. It was nothing I had experienced before. For the opening of the concert the host choir sang a song that was full of lots of actions. I had never seen that before. They expressed a lot of joy and you could see that they were having fun. The audience was just as happy. The night was filled with a mixture of different inspiring artists. I was glad I had gone. It was a wonderful experience.

I told Wade I wanted to get some songs like what I had heard at the concert, so we went to a music store to see what I could find. While going through the CDs I had no idea what I was looking for or what I should buy. I didn't know any of the artists or title of the songs. After searching through a lot of CDs I finally decided to take a chance. I picked a CD by an artist called James Hall. We went back to Wade's apartment. He put the CD in and the first song started to play. We both looked at each other and started laughing. We couldn't believe what we were hearing. The song that was playing was the song the choir had sung to open the concert. It was called "King of Glory". It was amazing! It was such a coincidence.

I was overjoyed with my new CD. There wasn't a song on it that I didn't like. It became my favourite music to listen to. I played it often. Certain songs were left on repeat for a period of time. Gradually

I started to add more CDs to my collection. I was enjoying listening to my new sound of music.

After a couple of visits to the church, I was reintroduced to the concept of baptism. To be baptized means that you are tired of your old life and want a new one. You want to become a new person, and this could be accomplished by first admitting that you haven't been living a life according to God's standards, and that you want to accept His Son Jesus Christ into your heart and life. After you admit to this, it is followed by you being placed fully into a pool of water (John 3:3-5, Acts 2:38). By doing this, you will receive a full cleansing and your slate will be wiped clean, because of Jesus dying on the cross. At the end of the service I heard the Pastor asking who would like to turn their lives over to God. I thought about it and I wanted to do it. I wanted to be baptized. I felt the need to do it all over again. I wanted to turn away from my old life. I knew I had had a change of mind and heart, and even my attitude was changing. I needed a complete turn around in my life.

After the service, I was speaking to some of the ladies of the church. I told them about my desire to be re-baptized. But because I had mentioned being baptized when I was a little girl, they said I didn't have to be baptized again. Even though they said it wasn't necessary I felt differently. I knew I needed to experience it all over again. I didn't know where to start from unless I did. Doing it again would enable me to start from the beginning.

Baptize Me

A short time after was the Easter service. The Pastor in his sermon spoke about salvation. Salvation is the gracious undeserved gift of God. He explained how God came into the world as Jesus, and died on the cross for us to have a relationship with Him. When we are in a relationship with Him we were guaranteed to experience a life of Him taking care of us, and keeping us safe and much more. He would enable us to have a better life, and someday if we continue the relationship with Him, we would live with Him in eternity. I believe it to be true. I wanted to live this life. After hearing this it made me feel more strongly about getting baptized. The following Sunday during the church's announcement they mentioned that the Pastor was available during the days if you needed to speak with him. I decided I needed to let him know I wanted to get re-baptized. I was so excited. I told Wade what I wanted to do. He was happy for me. I told him I was going on a journey, and it was up to him if he wanted to come along.

I couldn't sleep that Sunday night. All I could think about was getting baptized. The morning couldn't come soon enough. I still had to wait until noon because that's when the Pastor would be in the office.

Wade picked me up twenty minutes before noon and we went to the church. The Pastor was there. I was very relieved. We were led upstairs by the secretary to his office. As we entered his office he greeted us with a warm greeting. We spoke briefly about other things and then I got to the point of expressing my desire to be baptized. He was elated for my decision. He said it could be done on the upcoming Sunday. I was disappointed. I asked him if I couldn't be baptized that day. I told him of my excitement and not being able to sleep, and I thought I would be baptized right there and then.

Seeing my disappointment, he said he would have to see which of his leaders would be available to baptize me. I found out that he wasn't the person who did the baptism. He made a couple of calls and after he gave me the good news. One of the leaders would be able to baptize me, but I would have to return later in the evening. I didn't mind. I was excited that it was going to take place that day. I thanked the Pastor and we left to return later that evening.

I called Momma at work to give her my good news, and see if she would be home in time to come and see me get baptized. She said she would. Wade and I and Cassie along with Momma went to the church at the time given by the Pastor.

When we got there sister Whalen was also there, which was a nice surprise along with a couple of other ladies who were active in the church. They spoke to us for a short period of time expressing how elated they were that I was getting baptized.

One of the ladies, who I had become friendly with was sitting beside Wade, and speaking to him about getting baptized. I noticed that he had tears rolling down his face. This was surprising. I had never seen Wade cry before.

Sister Whalen asked Momma if she wanted to get baptized, and to everyone's surprise Momma said "Yes". We both got changed and heading for the pool that was already occupied with the leader who was going to baptize us. I remember the leader held my hands together as we stood in the water and he gently brought me underneath the water. As I was coming out of the water I felt this feeling come over my body, I can't explain it, except to say that I felt refreshed. With each passing day following my baptism I felt as though I was coming alive spiritually. I had been given a new life. I was happy that I had surrendered my life to Jesus. It was a night I would never forget. (Cassie, a year later would decide that she wanted to be baptized, and a few years after our baptismal, Jake would visit our church and also decided he wanted to get baptized).

I started to go to the gym with Wade, and reading my Bible all the time was my new found delight. I would go on fasting, which was times I chose to go without food or anything to drink, and my focus was on prayer and reading my Bible. I was hungry to know more about my new found life, and about the God I was reading about in the Bible.

Receiving the Holy Spirit

After my baptism I was told that I needed to receive the gift of the Holy Spirit. I had to speak in tongues. I remember as a little girl while living with Aunt Pat I would hear her speak in tongues and the people at the church too, so hearing about this was not new to me.

I was told one of the church leaders would come to my home, and pray with me to receive the Holy Spirit. We scheduled a day and time. Early in the morning the leader contacted me to say she was unable to come. I was very disappointed. I wanted to experience the Holy Spirit.

Speaking in tongues is supernatural. It is a Spirit inspired utterance and described as a free gift from

God given to the believer. The believer speaks in a language that they have never learned. It is a language unknown on earth. It is an initial outward sign that you have the Holy Spirit. It is also used by the believer to speak to God in his or her personal devotion for the purpose of praying, singing and giving thanks. It will help you build up your spiritual life. (Acts 2:1-6, I Corinthians 13:1, I Corinthians 14:1-28)

I had discovered for God so loved the world that He gave His only begotten Son was just the beginning of the love affair between a believer and God (John 3:16). Through His Holy Spirit each believer could have a direct encounter with Him, and an on going love experience, which would lead to the ultimate love relationship (John 14:16-18). His Spirit dwelling in us would give us guidance, and help us overcome weakness for strength, sorrow for joy, and peace for anxiety.

I learned that God reveals things to our spirit through the indwelling of His Spirit that our natural senses (eyes, ears) would never be able to sense. This does not mean that our natural senses have no importance. They are all needed and have a unique function in God's plan as our spirit, soul, heart, and body. God has given us the capacity to gain an accurate understanding of who He is. He illuminates our life in the Spirit. We are led by the Spirit (Romans 8:14).

I decided to go in prayer by myself to receive the Holy Spirit. I started praying while trying to remember what I had heard others say in order to receive the Holy Spirit. After some time in prayer, I began to notice that what I was trying to say was not coming out exactly the way I intended. I kept trying to correct my words. But it wasn't working. The more I spoke the more my words were unrecognizable. Finally I realized that what was coming out of my mouth sounded like tongues, but then that changed and sounded Asian. I was so shocked! "What is going on, I thought?" "Was this really happening?" "Was this coming out of my mouth?" So to make sure, still on my knees, I crawled over to my dresser mirror to look at myself. It was definitely coming out of me. I couldn't believe it! No one told me that this would happen! I had no idea what to do. I called Wade. I tried to explain to him what was happening. Our conversation was partly comprehensive. He was elated for me. He told me to call sister Whelan. I searched frantically for her number. I found it, and was very relieved that she answered the phone. I quickly tried to explain what was happening. She told me that she would stay on the phone with me and that I should keep worshipping God. Next thing, I heard the Pastor on the phone with us and they were both encouraging me to keep worshipping. With both of them on the phone I felt free to worship as they worshipped with me. The more I worshipped the more the tongues were flowing out of me. It seems as if we were on the phone for hours. Then gradually it subsided. Ever so often when I spoke, my sentences would be mixed with tongues. This would continue all through the day. The Pastor and sister Whelan were praising God for what He had done. I had received the Holy Spirit! Later in the day when I saw Wade, I tried to explain my experience and how I felt. It was unexplainable. I could only compare it to having a feeling like I could do anything. I felt as though God was right there. I didn't think I was explaining myself very well except to say that it was something he had to experience for himself. I was taught that I needed to see something before I should believe it. But, I discovered that the things pertaining to God were the opposite. You had to believe them first before you could see or receive.

Things no Longer the Same

My relationship with Wade changed in the following weeks after my experience. Whenever he tried to kiss me I told him I couldn't. It was no longer possible for us to have the same relationship as before. I ended being intimate with him. He said he understood that my life was changing, but didn't agree that our relationship had to change. I knew according to my new found faith that it did. He brought up the fact that I had agreed to marry him within a year. It so happened that all my changes were taking place around the time I was to give him my answer whether or not I would marry him. I did give it some thought, and I did want to marry him, but this was before all the changes. I thought we were a good fit. Whenever we went out people would comment on what a beautiful couple we made. This was a very hard decision. I came to the conclusion that I had to do what I felt was right for me. I had to see where this new life was going to lead me.

Wade wasn't ready to get baptized. To live the same life as I thought I needed. We weren't on the same page or the same path. Our relationship came to an end. I knew he was a special guy. The thought of letting him go was scary. I didn't know what was down the road, or if I would ever come across another guy who loved me as much as I felt he did. Whenever I looked into his eyes I could always see the love he had for me. Whether I would see this look again only God knew.

I couldn't allow myself to think about what I was leaving behind. I had to keep moving forward. I was fed up of the life I had been living. I was tired of the men, dancing and taking off my clothes. I was tired of drinking, drugs, and the club life.

After I was baptized, I made the decision to become a member of the church. I was on a new journey. I gave up dancing all together. I knew it was no longer a part of my lifestyle. I felt my life had been going in the wrong direction, for a very long time. I was delivered from despair, free, lighter, and happier. I had been given a fresh start. I felt at peace with my new life. I had found hope for life. Whom the Son sets free is free indeed! My life was starting over.

CHAPTER NINE

Starting Over

*"Therefore if any man be in Christ, he is a new
creature: old things are passed away;
behold, all things are become new."*
(2 Corinthians 5:17)

With my new faith, and church, my life had taken a 180 degree turn around from where it was. I was no longer going from place to place or from one relationship to another. Neither was I drinking, and getting high trying to fulfill my needs. I was living a clean and sober life, and I loved it.

Great Expectations

I quickly found out there were a lot of changes that Cassie (who was ten) and I would be expected to go through. One of the changes was in our clothing. We were no longer allowed to wear pants, which was pretty much all of our wardrobe. I didn't have many dresses, and what I had were certainly not appropriate for me to wear to church.

I had to go on government assistance until I found a job. The skills I had required were not useful being apart of this church. I had to find a job that didn't acquire me to work in a bar or work as a cosmetician. I found out that we were also not supposed to wear make-up either. I knew if I didn't wear make-up, I couldn't work in that environment applying it or selling it to others.

I had to swallow my pride and go to a place called the Thrift shop. Someone had told me about this place. It was where I would be able to find clothing at an affordable price. They were considered to be gently used clothes. This was the store's way of saying that although the items were previously owned by someone else; they were still in good condition. I found this to be ironic, because for years I used to donate clothes when they called from different charities looking for gently used clothing. I walked down the isles to see what I may find for me and Cassie. I was thinking as I searched through the many racks of clothing how ironic it would be to come across an item I may have donated.

I felt very uncomfortable being in the store. In that moment I was hoping that I wouldn't run into anyone I knew. I would be humiliated. How would I explain my being there? I never thought I would be in such a place shopping for used items, especially looking for clothes. I felt more embarrassed having Cassie with me.

I tried to stay focused on the fact that if we wanted to fit into our new church we would have to suck it up and do what was necessary at the time. We got a number of items and quickly left the store.

I threw out all my jewellery, my make-up and all my CDs, which were non-Christian. I had to take my braids out. They were frowned upon at our new church. It came in the form of preaching or someone walking up to me to say "You're not supposed to do that you know!" I started to emulate the look of those around me. I tried to drill into Cassie all the things that were not acceptable. Because I wanted to change my life from the way I was living I was going to make sure I followed all the rules and regulations. I wanted us to be accepted and fit in.

I soon found out that no matter how I dressed the part, and carried myself, I would still be placed in a category as a single woman with a daughter out of wedlock. I was categorized in the single mothers' group. This group I thought were treated in a negative way. We were single mothers struggling with many issues. I felt like an outcast amongst the rest of the members of the church. There were a couple of us who bonded because of this very fact. We became a source of support for each other. When one of us were in need, we would seek out help amongst the rest whether it was emotionally or financially. One of the young ladies and I became good friends. Her name was Mary. As we went along in the relationship she became a mentor, sister and at times maternal. We did a lot together. We were like two peas in a pod. At times we travelled out of town, and out of the country visiting other churches and conferences. We spent hours on the phone in conversations being silly, like high school girls. We both enrolled in Bible College at the same time, and helped each other out with our assignments. Both of us encouraged each other when things got tough, especially financially. We prayed, and cried together, but we also laughed a lot together.

Educating Myself

Going to Bible College was something I felt I needed to do. I was happy that I was going to learn more about what I was reading in my Bible. I thought it would give me a better understanding of the God of the Bible.

The Bible College was through my church, which was very convenient. I went once a week. If you knew what degree you wanted whether bachelors, masters or doctorate you were able to branch off later after the prerequisite courses. In the beginning I was only taking the courses for knowledge.

It was while spending time reading my Bible; I was drawn to one of the women characters. The

Bible refers to her as "The woman of Samaria". Because of her simple status, and her lifestyle, the Samaritan woman went to the well in her town for water during the hottest time of the day to avoid running into people from her town. It is at this well that she meets Jesus, Who had a lengthy and candid dialogue with her. She was impressed that Jesus knew all about her not so good lifestyle, and she admitted to Him, her wrong choices and misdeeds. The woman had a change of heart and mind. Her spirit was enlightened, accelerated, and illuminated by Jesus. After her amazing encounter with Him, the woman goes back to tell her family, friends, and neighbours. She broadcasted her experience of how she met Jesus and how He revealed His knowledge of her wrong doings. He offered to give her what she needed, what she was craving. That He could change her life, and give her eternal life. This woman, after her encounter with Jesus lead many people from her town to Him through her zeal and love for God (John 4:39–42). She had an impact on others by sharing her encounter. They believed her. They wanted to meet Jesus for themselves, and after meeting Him they believed in Him even more. They had had their own experiences with Him. The woman went to the well to get a jug of water. But instead she got much more including a cleansed and refreshed spiritual life. She is known as a great evangelist. I realized after reading her story, that God was showing me, that she was a reflection of who I was. Our lives were similar along with our powerful experience of meeting Jesus. I identified myself with her story. Jesus had met both of us right where we needed Him.

Almost a year had gone by. I spent most of my time studying the Bible. I hoped by reading the Bible it would lead me into a full encounter with Jesus and help me to experience His life. I wanted to hear His voice and obey His commandments. I was also learning to pray with purpose while in the process of looking for work.

My biggest request when I prayed was to find a job. It was very difficult financially. I was grateful for my parents who helped us out. At times Momma showed up at my house with bags of groceries, or Daddy had sent her over with a large bag of rice or potatoes with some kind of meat. It was always something we needed. My parents were great in helping me out during my rough times.

Receiving assistance from the government was hard. The money I received monthly only stretched so far. It was obviously created just to help you out for a short period of time, and I was well aware that the point wasn't to have people staying home and relying upon it. I have known people who were on it for a long period of time. I am not sure how they accomplished this. I found it quite difficult. There was such a stigma with being on assistance, and because of this, I never mentioned it to anyone except to some family members and close friends.

One day while picking up groceries at the Wal-mart close by my house, I ran into one of my best friend from my old neighbourhood. We were friends before I had met Jessie. She was working there with her boyfriend in the shoe department. We spoke for a bit, and I told her that I was in the process of looking for work. She said she would speak to her manager, and maybe he could hire me. I gave her my phone number, and she promised to give it to her manager.

A few days later, I received a call from a man that introduced himself as the manager of the shoe department at Wal-mart. He told me my friend gave him my number, and asked if I was still interested in getting a job in the department. I said "I am". He asked if I was able to come in that evening. I said "Yes."

Job Opportunity

I went to the store and met the manager; he said he could use someone for the evening shifts, and asked again if I was interested, and again I said "Yes." He asked if I could start that evening, but I told him I couldn't, because I had a daughter. I had to make proper arrangements for her. He told me I could start the next day instead. I thanked him for the job, and said I would return the next day.

I was in high spirits. I was thankful that my prayer had been answered. My shift was in the evenings during the week. I was happy I no longer had to stay on assistance. With my new job and a house that was rented according to income I would be independent again.

I called Momma and told her my good news. I asked if she could stay with Cassie the next evening. She agreed and was happy that I had finally gotten a job.

The next day, I showed up on time, nervous to be starting a new job. I met with the manager. My friend's boyfriend was also there. I would be working the evening shift with him. After filling out a few new employees forms I was well-informed as to my new job requirements. I was given a tour around the store and the department. My friend's boyfriend was also Jamaican, and I guess sensing my nervousness he put me at ease with funny comments as we made our rounds.

My shift went by quickly that night. It was a good feeling to have a job again. I was happy it didn't involve removing my clothes.

After working for a period of time Cassie and I had the discussion about her staying home on her own. She was now twelve years of age. It was decided that while I was away at work she would be good on her own. I was only ten minutes away. But it was still a hard decision to make. I thought her big size dog, which was by her side with her every movement, would be good company. With phone calls from Grandma, her Dad, and myself I thought it would work.

Angels on Earth

There were times I was sure I had encountered Angels. One day, I decided to go by the water to sit and read my Bible. As I sat by the water, a man came up quietly a few inches away, and stood looking out on the water. I glanced at him briefly from the corner of my eyes, and returned to reading my book. He was dressed casual, but nice. He stood there with both hands behind his back. A few minutes went by, and then he said "Are you reading the good book?" I turned and looked at him with a smile and said "Yes I am" He smiled at me, and turned his attention back to looking out at the water again and then he walked away. I turned and watched him as he walked away. He continued to stroll along with his hands behind his back until he was no longer visible to me. His presence, and the manner in which he spoke left a lasting impression, which made me feel I had been in the presence of an Angel.

I thought I had another encounter with an Angel, while working during the Christmas Season. The store was open twenty-four hours. My shift was working through the night. At three o'clock in the morning a man passed by my department. This was surprising, as no one was shopping at that time. The only shoppers I had seen were a couple that obviously had been out drinking, because they were noticeably intoxicated.

He said "Hello" and asked how my night was going. I responded that it had been quiet. He continued to ask about my job and what led to me working there. We talked about my new life as a believer of Jesus Christ, and how I hoped to make a difference in the lives of others. It was a stimulating conversation. He had a pleasant demeanour, attentive and very interested in what I had to say. After he bid me goodbye and walked away I realized the conversation had been focused on me, therefore I had no information about him. In his presence I felt lively and free to share things about myself, which didn't happened too often. This made me believe I had encountered another Angel.

My next encounter took place while traveling to work on a bus. I was sitting reading my Bible, and a man sat down beside me. I glanced at him to notice that he was an elderly man. The way he was dressed reminded me of the styles from the thirties. Still looking into my Bible I heard him say "Are you reading the good book?" I looked over at him and smile and said "Yes I am" and that was it. I continued to read my Bible, and got off the bus a couple of stops later. Once again it was his presence and the fact that he asked me the same question as the man by the water. These incidents and the way I felt during and after being in the presence of these men is something that has never left me. I thought surely they were not just coincidences. I like to think they were not. The Bible says "We ought to be mindful of strangers, because we could be entertaining an angel unaware" (Hebrews 13:2) (Paraphrase).

I remember being asked what were my hopes and dreams. What were my goals or plans for my life? They were questions I couldn't answer. I didn't remember having any dreams of what I wanted for my life. I hated thinking about what I wanted to be. I didn't know. I just knew I wanted a better life. I wanted a life that was filled with love and joy. It scared me when they would say "If you fail to plan, you are planning to fail" (Benjamin Franklin). I knew I didn't want to fail. I didn't have a plan. Coupled with other factors, one of the major influences was because I spent so many years waiting to die. I didn't envision myself being alive for a long time. I really didn't think I would live pass my thirties.

Now having been working at Wal-mart for four years I had a desire for further improvements to my life. I started to look into my options. I found out I had to return to school first in order to get my high school diploma before continuing any further.

Back to School

I also found out that there was an Adult High School for those who needed to obtain their diploma. I was anxious and scared about going back to school. It had been a long time that I had been to school. I thought I would need to go for a long period of time to achieve the credits I needed to graduate. After calling the Adult High school they instructed me to get my high school transcript from my previous high school. I did. I found out that I would be given extra credits for life experience. With these added credits I would only require a few more to graduate. I would only have to take a couple of classes for two semesters. I was very excited and relieved about this news.

I enrolled at the adult high school. Going back to school was a great experience. This was surprising to me. It was nothing like what I had envisioned. I met a lot of nice people. After completing my semesters I graduated with my high school diploma. It was a good feeling to complete all my classes and finally hold my diploma in my hand. It was difficult at times but I was glad that I had never given up and had push through to finish.

Having received my high school diploma I looked into going to college. I found out that I would be able to get a Student Loan from the government. My biggest decision was what field I would go into. I went back and forth between taking Social Work, Legal

Aid, and Office Administration. I finally decided to get a certificate in Office Administration. I thought with Office Administration I could work in any office with training.

I applied for the Student loan. I was approved. I was excited! With the loan that I would be getting from student loan I would be able to leave my job and focus on my studies while going to college full-time. I was thankful that my office administration course was only for one year.

Enrolled in secular college in addition to Bible College, which I had been going to for four years, became stressful. It was very different for me to be deeply involved in schooling. I never thought I would be going to two colleges at the same time and being a single mom. At times Cassie and I would be doing homework at the same time. My motto became "I can do all things through Christ who strengthens me." (Philippians 4:13)

During my second year of Bible College, I felt I should branch off to obtain my Bachelor degree in Evangelism. Evangelism is sharing the good news. To let people know that God loved them and He sent Jesus to die on the cross for those who would believe it and willing to have Him change them and their lives. I thought this was the area that best suited me. I wanted to share with others how Jesus changed my life. I wanted to share the good news of Christ's purpose on earth. I was drawn to this topic.

In Need of a Drink

I became overwhelmed by all that was required of me. One day, while at home and feeling over-whelmed and frustrated I suddenly had an urge for a drink. This was the first time since I had lost the desire for alcohol or drugs, that I felt this feeling. It had now been about six years. While I was having this experience Mary called me. I told her what I was experiencing. She told me in a loud voice to "Get out of the house!" In her voice there was urgency. I got off the phone and left the house and went for a walk. The feeling left me. It wouldn't be the last time I would experience this feeling.

After six years of attending Bible College, Mary and I both graduated with our Bachelors degree in our preferred Ministry.

I also finished my office administration course and received my certificate. I got the sad news that Mary who was working as the general secretary in our church, would be moving away soon to another city. The church was looking to fill the position not wanting it to be left vacant. Mary encouraged me to apply, and I did. I got the position. I had mix feelings. I was elated that I got the job, but would miss my dear friend.

I was grateful I was able to finish my courses for both colleges. It wasn't easy. There were moments I felt very tired physically and mentally. I knew I hadn't given up because of God. The weeks, months and years were hard at times. My experiences and difficulties brought a lot of frustration. I had changed, and was still changing by my dedication and consistency. During this period of starting over I was also going through the process of experiencing what it meant to be living a church life.

CHAPTER TEN

Church Life

After I had joined the church I found out there were many areas known as ministries to volunteer my time.

Working in Ministries

The first thing I was attracted to in our church was the choir. I wanted to sing. I have always loved singing since I was a little girl. I spoke to the choir director about my desire to join the choir. A few weeks later I was on the choir. I would be placed to sing with the sopranos. This section of the choir sang the high notes. I was very nervous at our first choir practice and even more nervous the first time I had to sing in front of the church. I wasn't sure how I would sound but I knew I couldn't be that bad. I was very excited to be apart of this choir. The choir was in need of a secretary and I volunteered. Our practices could be long at times. I knew they were necessary. I didn't mind because they were fun. During our practices it gave an opportunity for the members to bond with each other. The choir always sang at some point during our Sunday morning service. It was a good feeling to see the church members rejoicing with us as we sang. It made all those long hours of practices worth it. During our practices I learned a lot about music. I never thought I could memorize so many songs. I did. I loved singing the songs we learned. They made me feel really good inside. At times our choir travelled when we received invitations from other church conferences or concert in and out of town. Sometimes it could be out of the country. On occasion we stayed overnight in a hotel. Most of the time, we drove back to our own church in time for Sunday service. We would be very tired that day. Being on the choir was a great experience.

After spending six years on the choir I felt it was time for a change. I joined the Usher Board, and became an usher. It was definitely different from being on the choir. I had to get used to being in contact with a lot of people face to face. It made me feel more visible for some reason. I felt as though all eyes were on me. There was a lot of freedom walking up and down those isles seating people, and helping them with whatever their needs were. I stayed in this ministry for five years.

While being a part of the Ushers' ministry, I joined the intercessory prayer group. This group met for prayer at different times throughout the month. We prayed for all sorts of request. I loved praying. I felt as though I was making a difference when I prayed for others. Later, I also joined a youth prayer group.

One thing I found out was that you couldn't be bored at church. There was always something to do if you desired. I enjoyed filling in wherever I could, whether it was serving meals to members of our church when we had a conference or cleaning the church.

After seven years, I was ordained a Missionary. I was excited to be a part of this ministry. However, as I went along, I became increasingly discouraged about not feeling we were being effective and active in our community. I was disappointed at some of the road blocks we came across.

I saw there was a great need for us as believers to reach out to those in the community, but it seemed as if we were not doing enough or in the right places to be making a difference.

I used to wonder how I endured as a member in my first church. Our calendar was always full with activities. We had prayer service on Tuesdays, Bible Study on Wednesdays, Bible College on Thursdays, Youth service Fridays (which I went occasionally) and choir practice on Saturdays if there were no events scheduled for that weekend.

There Must Be More Than This!

Later, I became weary of the routine and my life. I was unhappy. I felt as though I was missing out and unsatisfied. I saw my life as not fulfilling. There had to be more. I had to take a good look at what was really happening. It occurred to me that my life was without balance. Having a Church life was great but I didn't have a social life. It was important for me to have a balance between my spiritual and natural life.

When I thought about it, most of my time was spent going to work, and then church, or meeting with other members of the church to pray and nothing else. There is good tired and bad tired. I felt I was experiencing bad tired.

I thought surely I didn't have to be doing every-thing spiritual. I believed in my heart that God wanted me to have some balance in my life. I knew we were spiritual, but also natural beings. I needed to find a balance for both.

I heard people quote the verse of scripture that says "Occupy til I come" (Luke 19:12-13) to jus-tify being busy in ministries, and not having time for anything else. I disagreed. I personally needed to have a balance life. I found myself after awhile questioning "Is this all there was?" Any vacation time was spent going out of town or country to a church conference. There was no real vacation. I thought how nice it would be to go on vacation and lay on a beach somewhere. It never happened. I never felt free to relax that way. Vacation time was still church time and this was my life.

I came across many people over the years that had everything revolve around church. It seemed as if not doing anything pertaining to church came down to the fact that you were not serious about your Christian walk. I have seen people working in ministry, and you could see the strain, and fatigue of not having any balance in their lives. It was obvious that they were not happy. There was something missing.

We weren't allowed to go to the theatre. Not wanting to be disobedient to the rules of our church, we rented movies instead. Cassie and I spent our spare moments watching movies. We purchased movies and started building a movie library. We had a lot of fun creating our favourite meals and watching movies. It was one of our mother and daughter bonding moments. Spending Thanksgiving holidays and Christmas with my family was my highlight. As Cassie got older and got a job her social life increased. With the rest of the young people of our church she participated in the activities that were planned. I thought she actually had more of a social life than I did. I was happy for her. I couldn't understand why my friends and I didn't have a social life. We never got together, to do things that I thought friends should do. Whenever we got together it was always church related.

Things became harder after Mary moved away. And a few years after when Cassie got married and moved to another city, it got worst. I felt very isolated and lonely. I would weep and complain in prayer before God. There were times I had people around me, but I felt alone. I thought there was something seriously wrong with me. I would ask God "Why did I not have a life like others?" "Why was I not enjoying my life?" "Where was the joy He promised me?" I found myself dangerously thinking I had a better social life when I wasn't in church.

After awhile I found myself moving towards a place of depression. Whenever I was at church or work I wanted to go home. I couldn't wait to go home to bed. I wanted to be by myself. I became an introvert with each passing day. My favourite thing to do as I got home was to change into my pyjamas and get some food and head straight into bed. The TV got turned on to a favourite show or I would pop a movie of my choice in the DVD player. After a period of time of this routine, I knew I wasn't in a healthy frame of mind. I began to have feelings of resentment. Things had to change. I had to take time out for other things. It wouldn't be given. It had to be set aside in order to have a balanced life.

Slowly, I started to learn to enjoy being by myself without feeling depressed about it. I thought about things that I could do to make me happy. I bought boxes of puzzles with beautiful sceneries, and made a list of places I wanted to go. I went to the beach a lot in the summer time. Being by the water was my favourite thing to do. Water brings peace and tranquility to me. I spent hours sitting on the rocks enjoying the atmosphere, which was peaceful. I loved going on long walks, and greeting new people as I travelled along the path ways

A Place of Balance

Eventually, I felt God was leading me to leave my previous church. When I did, there was a major difference in my personal life. This was a period of many transitional moments. My new church would be the place where I started to come into myself. I went to a lot of social events that were not church related. In doing so I met new people, and learned a lot from them. This was a refreshing change for me. I was happier, enjoying life, and learning to take in every moment. I had to learn that just because every waking moment wasn't in prayer or reading my Bible wasn't something I needed to feel guilty about. No longer having any restrictions about my wardrobe, I felt free to take part in many activities.

The first time I went rock climbing; it was very invigorating. Upon completing my climb to the top I had a feeling of accomplishment. Had I had the same restriction on my attire I wouldn't have experience that moment. I also enjoyed bowling and mini putting. I later planned these activities as outings for my family. These moments were a lot of fun and an opportunity of bonding time for me and my family.

Finding a balance does not mean trying to have things fifty-fifty. I think it is prioritizing what God wants me to do in a particular season of my life. I had to address the things that were of utmost importance first, but find time to take a break. I had to make time to go places that I enjoyed like the Arts Centre to watch different forms of dancing or a jazz club to listen to beautiful music. Taking part in activities, as these brought out the very best in me. They were adding to who I was becoming. It was in my best interest and even others around me, to find a place of balance in my life. I couldn't completely be me if this wasn't so.

God continues to help me to find a place of balance between my spiritual and natural life as I go along, to no longer feel condemned for wanting to enjoy the things He has surrounded me with. They are there for me to enjoy. It is His will that I do enjoy this life while I am here. He doesn't expect me to focus on just living a church life, and neglect my natural man, or visa versa. I need that balance to live this life as a shining light.

I believe because a lot of believers don't have a balanced life or see the need to have one; they tend to be unhappy believers. They are walking around with their light very dim. If I am not trying to live a balanced life my light will dim, which causes others to look at me as a believer who is unhappy. Jesus said that He came to give us life and more abundantly (John 10:10). He is a God of joy unspeakable and full of glory. I believe His word to be true. Each day my focus is to try and find balance in my life. Not to let the spiritual or the natural part of my life suffer in anyway.

I know it is imperative for me to feed my spiritual man, and to focus on having a deeper relationship with God, to seek to fulfill His purpose for my life. I also believe because God has blessed me with family and friends, He expects me to spend quality time with them, and not to neglect them because most of my time revolves around being busy with church matters.

The way I live my life is a witness of Jesus Christ to those around me, especially to those who haven't yet received Him into their lives. I often see a believer who is not portraying a good example or witness of what the message of salvation is all about. I think if we look so unhappy, why would anyone who is not a believer want to be one if they see no difference between their lives and ours. I think in order for us as believers to be true believers, without pretending we have a perfect life, we need to strive to find a balance. Each day we are living in hope knowing that no matter what, God makes the difference. This I believe would show us to be true witnesses for Him and the Kingdom.

I am growing spiritually, and maturing naturally. Therefore going to different places, experiencing different things is allowing me to understand the importance of being in tune with God. Discovering what my gifts, talents, likes and dislikes are enables me to learn more about myself. I found out that I am a creative person. I am most in my element when designing or creating something. When my creative juices are flowing I enjoy the use of colours, whether it is applying make-up, decorating, changing the theme colours in my home or clothing myself.

Being able to serve as a believer within or out of my church, in whatever ministry God wants me to be apart of, is something I am grateful for the opportunity to do. I am enjoying the journey of finding ways to find a balance in my life between ministry, work, and play.

In the process of keeping active, being consistent, faithful, and working in the ministries of the church, I would experience what would prove to be a very difficult and challenging time in my life. I call it being in the refiner's fire.

CHAPTER ELEVEN

The Refiner's Fire

*When you are joyful, be joyful; when you are sad,
be sad. If God has given you sweet cup,
don't make it bitter; and if He has given you
a bitter cup, don't try and make it sweet;
take things as they come – Oswald Chambers*

To refine, be refined or refining means to bring to a fine or a pure state; free from impurities: to purify from what is coarse, vulgar, or debasing; make elegant or cultured.

In the Bible, the process of refining metals is used as a metaphor. If something is made of pure gold or silver it is made from leftovers. In the process of refining everything else is removed, but only the metal that's pure remains. This is done successfully through firing and putting the metal over the fire until it liquefies, then the dross is able to be drawn.

The purification of precious metals by fire removes all impurities that would hinder the metal from becoming all that it should be. God supervises this process over our lives. We are sent into the fire by Him and taken out according to His satisfaction. The end result is for His glory.

As believers, we can get weighed down by our own desires, and ambitions, which hinder us from reflecting God's desires or reflecting His Image and Glory. He uses adversity, trouble, rejection, and failure to bring out the best in us. These afflictions we encounter and perceive to be bad are used to shape and mould us into the likeness of Jesus Christ.

I heard a story sometime ago about a lady who visited a silversmith to understand fully what it meant in the Bible verse "And He shall sit as a refiner and purifier of silver" (Malachi 3:3).

The lady went to see the silversmith without telling him the real reason why she was there. She asked him "What was the process of refining silver?" Which he preceded to described to her fully.

After he had finished explaining she said "But Sir do you sit while the work of refining is going on?" "Oh, yes madam" replied the silversmith "I must sit with my eye steadily fixed on the furnace for if the time necessary for refining be exceeded in the slightest degree the silver will be injured."

As the lady was leaving the shop, the silversmith called her back to make one final comment. That he only knows when the purification process was completed, by him seeing his own image reflected in the silver.

Even though we are placed in the furnace, Jesus' eyes are fixed firmly on us while the purifying work is being done. The trials that we will pass through are not accidental. When He is able to see His image within us then the purification work will be completed.

Between the sixth and eighteenth year as a believer, I experienced my greatest testing and trials. I found out that my expectation and perception of what could take place within and out of church was far from reality.

During those years, it seemed my testing and trials intensified with each passing year. I had entered a season, which seemed as though it had a beginning and no ending. It was during this season that my faith in God and everything else I knew to be true was put to the test. I later discovered it was my wilderness journey. It was a lonely, painful and dark place. I kept waiting for the light at the end of the tunnel to appear.

All this took place around the same time of the death of Mary. Her death left me with an experience of the greatest regret I have ever experienced in my life. The pain that came with her passing jolted and shocked me. It was as if I couldn't breathe. I felt lost after her death. I relied on her for many things in my life. I now found myself in a place where I asked "What do I do now?" "Where do I go from here?"

It happened one night when her son, my now son-in-love was over at my house. He and my daughter were to be engaged in the upcoming week. This was to take place in the city where Mary was living at the time. Her son was on the phone speaking with her before we left. We had made plans to visit my parents. Now at the end of the conversation with her, he turned towards me and asked "Would you like to speak to her?" I said "No" "I will see her soon" I thought we would have lots of time to catch up the following week.

Death of a Friend

A couple of days later, I received a call that she had passed away. I would forever find it hard to explain how I felt at the loss of my friend. I couldn't comprehend this news. It was unbelievable to me. I didn't understand how it could have happened, it was too soon. I was devastated. The worst feeling came with the regret of not speaking to her a few days earlier. I didn't know it would have been the last time I would hear her voice.

It took me a long time to forgive myself for not taking the phone that night, and even longer to get over the loss of Mary from my life. Sometimes I found myself thinking how things may have been if she was still here. Our children had married each other. We would be family and grandmothers together. I thought how she would love and get a kick out of our grandson. I call him the "Little Prince". I had to release myself from the place of regret and move on. I learned a lot of lessons from this experience. I vowed after to seize every moment and opportunity that came my way, and to value those in my life and those I came across.

Going Through a Rough Patch

During this season, it felt as though the bottom had dropped out from under me. My relationship with Cassie, which was always very close, went through a rough patch. It was a period of hard testing with misunderstandings. Things were said within and outside the relationship. We grew distant from each other. The day of her wedding made me feel as though I was watching from the sidelines as a spectator as opposed to being a participator. It was a very painful time.

There were people with their own input, which kept adding salt to my already open wound. The accusations and misconstrued reports made me feel as though I was losing my mind. It seemed as if hell had opened its mouth and was determined to swallow me up. I thank God for those family members and a dear spiritual mother who helped me through this time. They helped me to stay grounded and sane. I had people whispering in my ear as to why I wasn't walking her down the isle. It never occurred to me. I was happy her dad was around to do this honour. Their comments stirred up emotions inside me. I was determined that I was going to make the best of that day and take as much memories from it as I could. With this determination I was glad to be surrounded by family. Most of my family members had no idea of what I was really going through. I realized that all those years of being a single mother made me pour all of my heart and soul into taking care of Cassie. My life revolved around her. I had made her my everything. She was precious. She was perfect. One of the lessons I learned through our rough patch was that sometimes we place great expectations on others and ourselves. We expect smooth sailing in all our relationships, but as humans we will make mistakes. We will hurt the ones we love. Our journey with each other may come across pitfalls, but it will endure those rough patches. I learned never to put anyone upon a pedestal. Only Jesus should be put in that place. He is the only one Who is perfect. It was a hard lesson, but I learned it. I thank God that He restored our relationship over a short period of time, and our relationship has grown stronger through the years. I now refer to her as my daughter, sister, and friend.

My experiences have taught me that family, friends, leaders etc. will fail and disappoint you. But God cannot and will never fail. The Bible says "Put not your confidence in man" and I have learned this to be true (Psalms 118:8).

A couple of years after the death of Mary, I would experience the ultimate death that I always dreaded. It would be the death of a parent.

The Loss of the Pillar

Daddy would pass away two days after my birthday. The last time I spoke to him was at the hospital on my birthday. While visiting him, Momma reminded him that it was my birthday. She said "Are you going to sing her happy birthday?" and he sang happy birthday to me. That was a special moment.I will never forget it, first to hear Daddy singing after such an ordeal, and to have him sing happy birthday to me.

He had been sick for a few years, but with each passing one he became worse. Towards the end, I could see that being sick was beginning to take a toll on him.

It was hard seeing Daddy in the intensive care unit hooked up to so many machines. At one point his features changed because of all the water he was retaining and medications he was on.

I remember while he laid there I rubbed his head and told him that I loved him, and that God loved him. I had heard that the last thing to lose when someone was dying was their hearing. I wanted Daddy to know that we were there with him and we loved him. I told him while he laid there to open up his heart to God.

It was a difficult time for our family especially Momma. We were at the hospital every day for weeks while Daddy was in a coma. The day came when we had wonderful news. Daddy had awakened. He had slowly started to come around. It was like night and day when he came out of being under for many weeks. He had no recollection of all that had been going on around him. He seemed happy and thankful to God.

I remember standing at the foot of Daddy's bed. There was this moment between us. While others were talking our eyes met, and I felt as though he was looking at me with a knowing look. There was a twinkle in his eye. With that look a lot was being said. I felt in that moment there was an exchange of love that was being passed between us. Words can't explain how I felt seeing the look I saw in his eyes or on his face. The memory of that moment always stirs up joy in my heart. It was a great day. Unfortunately, this would only last for about a week. Once again, death would enter my life in a way that I hated it even more than before. I despised death.

I was at work when I got the call to come to the hospital. Daddy had taken a turn for the worst. I left work immediately. Many thoughts and scenarios were going through my mind as I drove to the hospital. I became fearful at what I might encounter.

Upon my arrival at the hospital, Momma and Kendal were already there. Deirdre arrived about the same time as I did. We were ushered into one of the quiet rooms. The doctor came in to inform us that Daddy wouldn't make it through the day. It was time for us to see him for the last time. It was time to say our goodbyes.

I knew this was It. We were told to call our Pastor and Momma did. This day would be one of the most painful days of my life. It was hard to see Daddy hooked up to so many machines again. For just a couple of days he had been free from them.

Standing over Daddy and seeing him laying there unresponsive felt as if I was having an out of body experience. All I could do as I rubbed his head and cry was to tell him that I loved him. I told him that he was a good father, and that I was grateful for him. It was hard to believe that this was it. I was saying good bye to my Daddy. I would no longer be able to ask him "How are you?" to hear him say "Not as good as you", and hear him tell funny jokes with a straight face. Or when we left the house, he would say "Call when you get home", or to hear him ask "Do you need anything?"

Throughout the day, we were in and out of the room occupied by Daddy. I remember at one point I went outside to get some fresh air. The sun was shinning brightly even though it was winter. It felt warm. I thought "How could it be so beautiful outside when upstairs my family and I were experiencing such a sad day?" My Daddy was lying upstairs on his way out of this life.

It was an emotional day. It was hard to see Momma experience losing her husband. She had known him for fifty-five years. I remember when Daddy came out of a coma he kept holding Momma's hand. He would call her by one of his pet names. It was a moment I wouldn't forget. They had been through many experiences in their journey together. In Daddy's final years Momma had become his nurse at home. Their relationship was until death do us part.

Finally, it came time to take Daddy off the machines, which were keeping him alive for us to spend time to say our goodbyes. The Pastor prayed and we all broke down crying. It was hard leaving the room and leaving Daddy behind. I knew the next time I would see his physical body would be at his viewing before his funeral.

We left the hospital and went back to our parent's home. It was more painful entering their home knowing I would never see Daddy again. It was hard to imagine never seeing him sitting in his favourite chair as I entered the house, or hearing his voice ask "Are you hungry?" knowing it was Momma who would prepare me something to eat. He was this way with all who entered their home. Daddy was the pillar of our family.

It was an emotional and painful experience, but we went through it together as a family. We had family members come from out of town, which was comforting. Our exchange of stories about Daddy brought laughter. We celebrated his life. I was honoured to read his eulogy at his funeral. It was good medicine for me. It took a long time to get over this loss. The hardest thing for me was getting up from where I was and moving forward. Moving forward to me meant moving forward without Daddy. This was very difficult to do. I knew Daddy would want us to be happy. That was the kind of family man that he was. With each passing day we all tried to move on with our lives. Until this day things happen to remind us of Daddy. It would make us laugh. He is alive in our hearts.

The Bible says "God is a Father to the fatherless" (Psalms 68:5) I had to look to Him to fill the void of the absence of Daddy.

These two deaths impacted me greatly. God is the only one who could have picked me up and helped me to move on.

Trying Times

During this period, I went through a lot of circumstances and situations where I experienced the mistreatment of others. This was a harsh reality. I came across people who attempted to make me feel terrible about who they thought I was. At times I felt the little bit of confidence that I had was being reduced. I wanted to disappear. The betrayal, disrespect and hurt from some, friends, family and church members were horrible. Their abusive words were hurtful. I thought I knew them. I considered them dear to my heart. These were the people I thought would be there for me, but instead ended up being against me. I found myself becoming a people pleaser even when they would hurt my feelings. The devastating thing was when I reacted to their mistreatment of me; I was accused of being "Sensitive." I think it was their way of covering up by placing the responsibility of their bad behaviour on me. It made me relate, and understand why some people walked away from their family members, friends and the church.

When I first went into the church, I refused to allow a hint of alcohol to touch my lips. It was a big deal for me. I made sure anything entering my body was alcohol free. The thought of any alcohol entering my body I felt, would contaminate it. During this time of emotional pain I struggled in silence with my afflictions. I desired a drink to numb the pain. I had to keep fighting the thoughts (which kept running through my mind) of how I would acquire a drink. But it never came to pass.

Because of these test, I felt God hated me. He didn't like me or love me. I thought He didn't know me even though the Bible said He knew me and loved me. I thought because of all the things I had gone through before coming into church, this should not be happening. I was in church! I was trying my best to live a life according to what I thought would please God. He couldn't know me. If He really knew me, He would make the excruciating pain and anguish I was feeling stop. I shouldn't be feeling this way.

I felt God was paying attention to everyone else but me. I thought some people were acting as if they weren't in church. They were doing whatever they wanted, when they wanted and how they wanted. I thought "Ok". I will just do things that I knew was considered not according to God's commandments. This would get His attention. I never could, because my conscience always got the best of me.

Most people I knew acted as if they were perfectly fine, they didn't need to be delivered from anything. They were living a very happy life. There was no one I thought I could relate to or felt free to confide in. I knew no one who remotely came from the same lifestyle that I had been delivered from. If they were, it wasn't known to me. I didn't want to be judged for my thoughts by those around me who I considered judgmental.

Sometimes, I felt like I was haemorrhaging on the inside but no one knew, they couldn't see. I remember feeling as if I had sunken into the ground and was covered over. All that was left was one of my hands reaching up through the ground. I was there waiting, hoping someone would see my hand and take a hold of it. No one did.

One thing I knew about myself was that, it was hard for me to pretend that I was fine when I was not. When I tried to hide how I felt, people noticed anyway because it showed on my face no matter how hard I tried. I remember on one occasion I was brought into a meeting with my Pastor and some of the leaders to discuss complaints about my demeanour. I wasn't asked what was going on with me, but instead given a list of what they saw that they thought was wrong with me. I didn't experience compassion in that meeting from those who were to be watchful over me, but instead I was met with accusations. I discovered that some people expect you to be at your best no matter what you are going through. You must put your best foot forward, and if you don't you are criticized. I believe this is what causes many to wear a mask. After this experience, I worked hard on putting myself together not to be brought into any more meetings, to hear their inputs on my behaviour.

I felt even more alone after this incident happened. This was a feeling I had hope would have changed with being a part of a church. Most of my life I felt like I was placed in a circle, and while in this circle I was able to reach out and touch others, but I could never come out of that circle, and no one could come in, not even my family or friends, they remained on the outside. It was me alone in this circle, and I was unable to come out.

A Need of Transparency, Take the Mask Off

Over the years, I heard preachers call out for those in the church to remove their mask. I agreed. I felt there was no transparency around me. I never knew the true testimonies of those in the church.

They would testify, but I knew it wasn't their real testimony. Their testimony was the sugar coated version or they told only parts of it. The people to whom I considered opening up to presented themselves as perfect. They made it seemed as if they had it all together. I thought the church was the one place that accepted imperfect people, and that was why we were all there. We were all there striving together to be moulded and shaped into better people. We wouldn't all be at the same level. Some people needed more time than others to go through the refiner's fire. I knew the only one Who was perfect was Jesus Christ Himself.

I believe the lack of transparency in our churches has caused tremendous upheaval and shameful circumstances among believers. It has caused confusion especially among non-Christians when devastating reports leak out about a Christian. I believe those who have been exposed hadn't been fully delivered from what held them in bondage. We need more people within the church to be more transparent with their struggles. When there is more transparency, those who are struggling will feel free to seek Godly counsel. They will not feel alone and struggle in silence. They will share their experiences with others. Experience speaks volume to me. It has always been my motto. Unless you have been through what I have experienced, you can only sympathize with me. That's as far as you can go. If you have been through a fraction of what I have experienced, then I will feel at ease to open my heart to you without feeling judged. It is the affective empathy or someone who has had a similar experience that people who are suffering will relate to.

Can I Die Now?

I got to the point where I hoped my life would come to an end. I wanted to die! The afflictions were imposing on me. Feeling this way was surprising. I never thought I would feel this way in church. I didn't have thoughts of committing suicide. Oh no! Instead I laid in bed thinking maybe I wouldn't wake up the next morning. Maybe God would answer me, and I would die peacefully in my sleep. All I was going through would come to an end. Finally it would all be over. But I kept waking up morning after morning disappointed. I thought "God, you wouldn't even do this for me." At times I said "Jesus how much longer I must endure my sufferings?" "Don't you feel sorry for me?" I used to think there must be many bottles with my tears stored up in Heaven (Psalms 56:8).

There were times I felt I was following Jesus' instructions to do certain things, or go certain places, but instead it left me experiencing rejection or being despised. This made me doubt and question if I had really heard God's voice in the first place. I wasn't sure He was leading me. I also found out that not everyone is happy for you when God changes you and turns your life around. There were people around me who allowed their negative feelings to overtake them when the gifts and talents God gave me started to come forth. It intensified when He showed His favour or blessed me. They tried to control me. They tried to tell me what I could do, and what I couldn't do. But God gave me the courage to stand up against them. This seemed crazy to me, because they were leaders in my church. I couldn't understand it. I thought this was why we were apart of the church.

A Mind to Live

One day while feeling down and discouraged. I came across a preacher speaking about someone needing to choose life in order to live. I realized at that moment this was God speaking to me. Unless I chose life, stop focusing, waiting, and expecting death, I will always be consumed with wanting to die. This would prevent me from wanting to live.

The thoughts of wanting to die continued to plague my mind. I was overwhelmed. I knew I had to stand up against the thoughts and not let them run freely through my mind. I had to fight! I knew this fight had to start in my mind. I had read Joyce's Myers book "The Battlefield of the Mind". This book spoke of the many negative thoughts we war with in our minds, and how we may over come them.

I knew I had to be determined in every part of my being that I wasn't going to go back to where I was coming from. I knew there were other options. One of them was prayer. I prayed with desperate cries to release my emotional pain, anger, and frustrations to Jesus. It had all been incubated for a long time.

Once I made up in my mind to live, it was as if I was able to think clearer. I started to see things differently. I knew I had to come into agreement with God and accept the fact that He loved me; that He wanted to make me better and as uncomfortable as my testing and trials were, they weren't there to kill me. Even though I was sure they would. I now understood they were there to make me better, to build me up, and make me stronger than I ever thought I could be. They were to remove some things, to make me more like Jesus. He wanted to bring things inside of me out. God wanted me to see that I was an over comer. I had that power in me. I was a conqueror, survivor, fighter, and born to win. I had to agree that God had chosen me to accomplish His will for my life, and I was full of purpose and potential.

The Truth of the Matter

Because of the rules and restrictions of my previous church, I raised Cassie very strict. I wanted her not to go in the same direction, or path that I had taken. I found myself apologizing to her years later when I discovered the rules, standards, and regulations didn't have to be so. Because I was willing to be obedient and happy to conform to the new lifestyle, I had become the parent I never wanted to be. I had become overprotective and at times controlling. I was the parent I had run away from.

It was while attending my new church Jesus impressed upon me that some things that people deemed important such as wearing pants, jewellery, or make-up were not things He cared about. He really cared about the state of an individual's heart. He desired relationship like He did with Adam and Eve in the Garden of Eden. There might be people who met the criteria on how one ought to look on the outside, but their heart would be far from meeting God's criteria. They didn't have a relationship with Him. He freed me from all those thoughts and gave me a different mind set. It wasn't instant, but the process was liberating!

Those who knew me prior to my liberation made remarks or gave their looks of disapproval straight on or by their side glances. They didn't understand my change. Their conclusions were that I had gone back to my old lifestyle, which was far from the truth.

One night, I went to a church to support an event. At the end of the night, I left disappointed. During the sermon the preacher mentioned the difficulty of differentiating between a believer and a non-believer because of their outward appearance such as wearing makeup. This comment was disturbing to me. What was more disturbing was the reaction of the people, especially those in leadership. They were supporting this mindset. I thought "In the times that we are living in this is the focus?" Never mind the many souls perishing!

I thought what about hearing the desperate cry of an individual and seeing the need of change for their lives. "What about leading them to Jesus?" He is the only one Who can set them free from a life of despair, destruction, and chaos. How about encouraging people, letting them know Jesus cares and loves them no matter what and wants a relationship with them.

As I listened to the preacher I thought "If I needed not to wear make-up, jewellery or pants for you to know whether I am a believer of Jesus Christ, that reveals more about you than me" "What about looking at the fruits of my life, as the Bible says?" (Galatians 5:22) "What is my life revealing to you about me?"

I am grateful that God has the final say whether or not I make it into Heaven. He looks on the inside out not on the outside in. It is the Spirit of God that changes a man from the inside outward not the words of another man.

I believe truth is known through our hearts or spirits rather than with our mind. That is why Christianity is past the rationalism of this world and directs you straight into that of a spiritual experience (Corinthians 2:9-10). It is beyond a list of rules, laws, or code of ethics that must be followed, but instead offers an express spiritual experience to know and encounter a loving God. Hearing Jesus is the first order of business. Prayer to know God's heart, joy, desires, hurts, character, will lead you on a pathway of spiritual experiences not legalism bondage. Relationship and spiritual intimacy is what is needed, not more theology about Him.

Through this I have learned not to approach people with justice and judgement. Jesus' approach is the ultimate example. He approached each individual with love, mercy, compassion, and then justice. I am thankful to God that the eyes of my understanding are being opened. I am delivered from that mindset. I am grateful I am no longer a clone of another person, which I was. I am on a journey discovering who I am, and the way God intended me to be and no one else.

Throughout the years, I felt as if I was being stripped away. I felt like I was being pruned or peeled layer by layer like an onion. It was emotionally painful. I had to come face to face with myself, with all my faults, and accept what I saw. I had to accept what needed to be changed, and allow God to make the necessary changes. It was going through these times I learned what it meant to praise and worship. I realized I had been given a gift to worship and dance. I learned God had not taken away my dance or my love for music. It was still there. My dance movements were different. They weren't for seducing men for money anymore. My dance was only for God in a way that was acceptable to Him. When I danced it brought joy, and freedom. I learned how to encourage myself and to depend on Jesus as my helper and deliverer.

Sustained and Provided For

In the process of all my experiences during my testing and trials I found out how much of a protector Jesus is. After driving for many years, in one year I experienced car accidents, which could have been fatal. The first happened one night after I had dropped a friend home. I left their street and pulled out unto the main road. I was driving along, and someone blink their lights at me. I thought maybe I had forgotten to turn my lights on. I checked. My lights were on. I proceeded and then a short time after, another car did the same thing. I kept driving. Suddenly I notice a car coming straight towards me in the same lane. It was then I realized what was going on. My mind was trying to process the car coming towards me. I was about to have a head on collision. Immediately I felt my car gently move over to the right side of the road. There were no abrupt movements. I kept moving along. The full realization of what had just happened started to sink in. I realized when I turned on the main road I had positioned myself in the other directions turning lane. The warning blinking lights from the coming traffic was to bring my attention to this fact. Because it was an extremely dark road I had no idea what I had done. I kept saying "Thank you Jesus!" over and over again. I prayed for the person I almost collided with. I was grateful. The outcome could have been fatal.

Another time, Deirdre and I were driving on a long stretch road. I was at the wheel. The speed limit was eighty kilometres, which you know you could push to one hundred kilometres. The truck ahead was going at a good speed. Suddenly for no apparent reason the truck's speed came almost to a stop. Because of the speed I was travelling I couldn't slow down fast enough. Not wanting to hit the truck I steered off to the gravel road on the right side. My car was heading for a large light post. I felt the wheel turn and brought my car back up unto the road. My car started to spin at this point in the middle of the road. It stopped right in the middle of the road side ways. It was then I noticed that another truck was coming towards us with speed. It seemed like a scene out of a movie. There was no time to get out of the way. My eyes were fixed on the front of the truck coming towards me and I said "Don't hit me!" The truck came to a stop. I straightened my car in the right direction to continue on our journey. Deirdre said "You did good!" I replied "It wasn't me" "It was God!"

My next accident made me feel as though I was in a scene from another movie. Early one morning I was driving to work. The road is usually very busy. As I was approaching an intersection I proceeded to slow down as did the cars before me. I came to a stop. I heard a noise. My car jerked, which made my body react. I knew I had been hit from behind.

I quickly put my car in park. I came out to see what damaged had been done. I saw a scene I didn't expect while moving to the rear. The young lady, who had occupied the car, was rolling out of it to the ground as I approached her to see if she was ok. Suddenly, I noticed her car was still moving! It was moving backwards down the street. I yelled while pointing in the direction it was rolling "Your car!" Without any hesitation I proceeded to follow her car. I tried to get in to stop her car. I made my first attempt but failed. I tried a second time, but it was very awkward trying to get in. I failed again. Finally, on the third attempt I was successful. I was able to get my foot in her car and positioned myself to place the gear in park.

I realized after hitting my car she had placed her gear in reverse instead of park. When she tried to exit her car, she fell out because it was still moving.

The young lady caught up with me and thanked me with tears in her eyes. I asked if she was alright. She responded that she was. We walked back to my car. I was relieved there was no sign of damage. She mentioned she was coming off work at a local grocery store. We exchanged our information. I told her to take care and left for work. A couple of hours later, I called to check on her. Her dad answered indicating that she was sleeping. He thanked me for calling to check on her.

I thank God for the way things worked out. Through the entire time that this scene was playing out, no other cars came our way to make things more complicated or dangerous.

During this time I learned how God sustains and provides. After four and a half years of working in the office of my church, I was laid off. It was surprising to me. I didn't expect it! I had to apply for unemployment insurance. The time allotted for me to collect that money ran out before I could get another job. Once again I had to go on government assistance. This time around I had a different attitude. I was grateful it was available. Not long after being on assistance, I was able to get another job working at an x-ray imaging clinic. I held the position as a medical receptionist. I also processed films taken by the Imaging Technicians.

After three years working for this company, I would be laid off. This time while laid off, my unemployment ran out and I made a difficult decision. I filed for bankruptcy. The credit card had not been over used by shopping expenditures, but from paying bills. I was grateful that I was still able to keep my car. After having my car for seven years it started to fall apart. I tried to see if I could get another vehicle. I had no problem getting around by the bus, but the truth be told, I had grown accustomed to having my own transportation. I went looking by faith not knowing what would happen.

After checking out some vehicles, I thought there was no way I could get what I wanted. I thought the prices were too high. There was also the issue of bankruptcy. I went through the motions as if I was buying a vehicle and changed my mind. I didn't know what I was going to do. Some weeks went by. I received a call from the dealership. It was the finance manager. He was enquiring why I didn't purchase the vehicle I saw. I explained my situation. He said he would be able to help me. He said the manager at the dealership was a friend, and would call him to help me find what I was looking for at a suitable prize. I agreed. A few days later as scheduled, I went to the dealership.

The first person I came across as I entered the dealership turned out to be the only car sales lady. She was a Christian and from Jamaica. I explained why I was there. She let the manager know I was there. While I waited she asked what type of vehicle was of interest. After a short time I was able to see the manager. I liked him. He asked the sales lady to help me find a vehicle. He assured me things would work out. Finding a vehicle seemed such a long process even though I had only checked out three SUVs. Anyone who truly knows me knows I am not a shopper. I have to set my mind I am going shopping in order to enjoy the experience. I like to go in a store, get what I want and get out. I knew buying a vehicle wasn't that kind of shopping. The second SUV I had chosen turned out not to be safe after it was checked. The manager indicated it wouldn't be safe, and couldn't sell it to me. It wouldn't be right. I had to check again. My third choice turned out to be the one I eventually bought. It had everything I was looking for and added features I didn't ask for, but was happy they were included. The manager gave me a good deal. He was extremely nice to me. I knew it was God's favour. My sales lady mentioned this fact. The manager wasn't just trying to sell a vehicle; he genuinely helped me to find exactly what I wanted and at a price which was affordable. I left happy with my truck.

Once again a week later after purchasing my truck I was laid off.

I was sure from past experiences God would take care of me. At times, I felt the fear of being out of work trying to sneak upon me. I had to hold on trusting God. My employment insurance ran out. I applied for assistance. During my time of looking for a job I decided to volunteer.

Turned Around

Thank God, the time came for me to be set free! God had smiled upon me. It was as if He had said "She has had enough, it's time to release her." Six months later, I got two job offers at the same time. They were both part time and didn't interfere with each other. My position at both jobs was as a receptionist. One job was working at a mechanics garage; the other was at a community health centre. After a month I had to let one go. It was extensive driving between both locations. But it worked out. I was able to get extra hours working at the community health centre. By the time my grandson was born and Cassie's maternity leave was over, I was available to take care of my grandson during the days while his parents worked. I went to my job in the evenings. I was happy the way things worked out.

After all the dust had settled, I discovered that I was stronger than I thought. The way God was changing me and my life was different than the next person. He works on each person according to their individuality and characteristics. I had to stop looking on other people's lives or measure myself by anyone else. But more importantly, that Jesus was with me and by my side through all my painful experiences. Just as Daniel wasn't alone in the lion's den or the Hebrew boys in the fiery furnace, Jesus was also with me in my fiery trials. He did encourage me during the silent times with songs or verses of scriptures. After this season of my life, it was becoming clearer that Jesus was showing Himself to be everything I needed and more.

One day, I went to visit another church. They were having a women's conference. On the third and final day of the conference, I knew Jesus was moving me to that church. I was grateful for the change. I knew it was time for me to leave my second church. I knew God wanted to do more in me and my life, and it wouldn't be accomplished where I was. While I was settling in my third church, I went to what they call "Encounter" I had been on retreats before where you are able to get away from it all, focus on God and your relationship with Him. It was a time to get reconnected with Him, to get deliverance from everything that was hindering you in your life from being all He has called you to be.

I felt I needed to go. My life had shifted. I felt battered after all I had been through. I had lost my identity through all the testing and trials. I was in a place where I needed to be reminded who I was, and what God's expectation was. I needed to know what was going on, and the next direction for my life? It was while going on this weekend of encounter, which was more than a retreat that I learned to forgive those who had mistreated, or offended me. I discovered that rejection was good for me. It made me stop and seek God's counsel to know it was time to move. Sometimes rejection comes from you sowing a good seed into a bad environment. Because it isn't a good environment for you, the seed cannot grow the way it should, so God has to remove you from that environment to another where you can bear and bring forth fruit.

Often we think we are waiting on God, but really He is waiting on us to keep following His instructions and directions. If it hadn't been for rejection I would have stayed comfortably where I wasn't fulfilling my full potential and purpose. But more importantly I found out that God was going to write me a new story.

CHAPTER TWELVE

A New Story

*The Spirit of the Lord GOD is upon me; because
the LORD hath anointed me to preach good tidings
unto the meek; he hath sent me to bind up the
brokenhearted, to proclaim liberty to the captives,
and the opening of the prison to them
that are bound;*

*To proclaim the acceptable year of the LORD,
and the day of vengeance of our God;
to comfort all that mourn;*

*To appoint unto them that mourn in Zion, to give
unto them beauty for ashes, the oil of joy for
mourning, the garment of praise for the spirit
of heaviness; that they might be called trees of
righteousness, the planting of the LORD, that he
might be glorified .(Isaiah 61:1-3)*

Writing this book was a major surprise to me. I didn't envision this. I thought I would share my testimony with other individual as I went along in my life. I didn't see myself writing out all the details of my life in a book for others to read. But the Bible says we overcome by the word of our testimony.

There has been different stages of my healing process, and writing this book was apart of it. It has been very therapeutic pouring myself out over these many pages. Even though Jesus had brought different ways to counsel me throughout the years of the traumatic events, which took place in my life, at times, writing my story was like going back to the scene of a crime. There were emotional times, and found myself weeping after I had written a particular chapter. A lot of tears were shed as I came face to face with my past, but after completing that chapter I felt relieved. The more I wrote the emptier and lighter I became, I felt like a bucket being emptied of its contents.

The process of transformation, which led me to my purpose was hard but necessary, and worth it. There were times when I wondered what I have done to deserve to end up in such a place. No matter how hard I tried to do well and live the best way I thought I should, things only got worst. I couldn't go around it, over it, or under it. I had to go through it. Through the years, I experienced many emotions such as sorrow, self-pity, frustration, anger, resentment, bitterness, doubt and fear, to name a few. I learned that holding on to these emotions were only holding me back. The sooner my attitude changed the sooner I would be able to move forward to my destination. It wasn't an easy thing to do. There were times when I felt tired of the ongoing, never ending process of letting go of some of my attitude towards change. I got to the place where I felt extremely broken, that the old Elaine had been stripped away. I felt as though I was standing naked and opened not knowing what was going to happen to me next? I discovered this was exactly the right place I needed to be in. I was yielded and giving total control of myself and life over to God. I was going to have to trust that He would take care of me.

It has been a long, rough, and painful journey, which I wish for no one. A journey filled of many lessons, trials, heartache and disappointments, but through it all Jesus never left my side. There were many days and years that it felt like He had abandoned me. Those times I felt betrayed, unloved and chastised by Him, but it was all for my good. You wouldn't be able to convince me of this fact at the time while I was going through my dry and desert place. I couldn't see the end in sight and felt completely hopeless, and lonely. I was desperate to get out! I was trapped, but no one noticed what was happening to me, instead they added to the drought of my life.

As I went along my journey, I did learn a lot about myself, life, and the people in it. The most important thing I learned was the reality of God. That His Mercy, Grace, and Love are real. I know because I experienced them. They have brought me to the place where I am now. They rescued me, changing me and my life. I thank God for not leaving me the way He found me, in the mess that I was in.

There were many changes in my life along the way. Some changes at the time weren't welcomed.

In the long run I had some understanding of why they needed to take place. It was good that I was afflicted (Psalms 34:19, Psalms 119:71). I learned to encourage, pray, and be a good friend to myself.

I thank God for my enemies. Thank God that He prepares a table before me in their presence (Psalms 23). He has not made me to be ashamed.

Shame and Guilt Removed

A few years ago, I called the Women Rape Crisis Centre to volunteer on their crisis line. I had to go through a three month training process to know how to handle the calls I would receive on my shift. I didn't realize at the time that by going there what a major impact it would have on me.

One of our sessions was how to handle calls from those who worked in the sex industry. It was as though a light bulb went on in my mind. All those years of dancing, taking off my clothes for money, I never saw myself as someone who worked in the sex industry. I thought being a dancer (stripper) was different than being a prostitute or escort girl. It dawned on me that there wasn't really any difference when it came right down to it. There were just differences in locations. I realized I had been an indoor prostitute. The services offered may have been different but it was still selling sex for money. It was just in a safer and controlled environment. The impact of being a part of the training was geared for me. I felt the purpose of me going there wasn't about being on the crisis line. It was to relieve me of all my guilt and shame about my past. I had been released. I had been set free. (*"But thou, O Lord, art a shield for me; my glory, and the lifter up of mine head." (Psalms 3:3)*

Forgiving all those who did me wrong was quick. It was forgiving myself that took longer. I had to come to the conclusion that some things that made me feel ashamed and guilty weren't entirely my fault. No matter what bad choices I may have made along the way, I owed myself forgiveness in order to move forward in my life.

As time went on, God taught me how to use things as stepping stones instead of allowing them to be stumbling blocks. I learned how to trust God while taking the steps. At times it wasn't easy. I had to keep reminding myself of His promises that He made to me, and also those written in the Bible. They were His Word.

There were times I felt God was taking too long to answer my prayers. Some prayers He would answer immediately. But there were those I thought were more important that came with no answers or deliverance. They seemed to take longer. Some prayers and promises I am still waiting for Him to fulfill. I know He will.

Many times I was unable to figure out what God was doing in my life. I felt distant from Him as though He had left me. But I found out after that He had always been with me. He had never left me or forsaken me. He was right there the entire time. When He is finished changing me into who He wants me to be, I would shine like a diamond.

Timing is a major thing with God. He manoeuvred me through all my testing and trials. All things worked out for my good, and are still working out for my good. He has been tremendously faithful to me. He has kept me through it all. I am overflowing with gratefulness. Thankfully He is the one Who is in charge of my destiny.

I remember after hitting rock bottom, I was seeking out for something more to my life. I didn't know exactly what I was looking for or what I needed. I remember watching the movie "The Bodyguard". There was a scene where Whitney Houston and her sister in the movie were singing "Jesus loves me." It was a different version from what I heard in Sunday school. After watching this movie I found myself singing this song over and over again. It stuck with me for a very long time. It became an anthem to me. Looking back, this song was one of many things I felt Jesus used to woo me back to Him.

I liked Whitney Houston. I remember when she first came on the scene. She was full of life and possibilities. I used to dance to her songs in the clubs. Therefore when she died, it affected me in a way no other public figured ever did. I cried. I think it was because I identified with her struggle. She was my age. I was on the sidelines routing for her. I wanted her to get back on track. I was hopeful her life would turn around as my life did. When it seemed as though she had lost the battle in this life, I broke down. I thought the ending to her story could have been mine. My life could have been cut short. But thank God Grace and Mercy was keeping me going.

Many years ago while leaving my job at the church; I was going to my car which was parked in the back. I came across a high school student smoking up weed. I was very familiar with that smell. I asked him "Why are you smoking up?" "Because my friends do" He said. I told him he might not like where smoking up may lead him. I found myself sharing a bit of my testimony with him. I told him I didn't know when I started drinking and getting high I would end up being addicted. That sometimes we are the last to know what we are really capable of whether good or bad. I told him that Jesus rescued me and changed my life.

I encouraged him not to follow his friends. He had a lot to look forward to in his life. He put his joint out, and thanked me. I told him to take care of himself. He walked away. My heart went out to him. As I sat in my car I said a prayer for him.

Many people hit rock bottom and don't recover. They lose the fight.

I was sharing a bit of my life story one day with someone. She asked me how I stopped drinking and getting high. I told her I lost the desire suddenly. This individual who is a nurse said "Do you understand what a miracle that was?" "I don't think you understand" she said. She continued to say as a nurse when someone is a substance user and abuser such as alcohol, they would have to be weaned off it slowly. They would be given small doses of alcohol not to let their body go into shock. It could kill them otherwise. Hearing this made me appreciate Jesus even more. I felt extremely grateful that He heard me, and answered me.

I never considered the consequences or the outcome of being sexually active or my endless usage of drugs and alcohol. Looking back, I realized how I ignored the physical pain I was encountering. I needed to numb the emotional pain that seemed far greater. People would say they were surprised I never got alcohol poisoning considering the way I used to consume alcohol at my weight and height.

Often I have been asked if I had to do it all over again if I would have left home. My answer has always been I am grateful for the woman I have become. I am grateful for my daughter. I am happy that she got married, which brought me a son, and the children that came immediately in my life with that union. I am blessed to have my grandson the "Little Prince" who came afterwards. If I was to change anything in my life, it may have altered the events leading up to how things are now. Looking back, I honestly have no regrets. Yes, better choices could have been made. But maybe things wouldn't have worked out the way they did.

I never went out of my way to tell people my age. While growing up I heard people say a lady never tells her age. But the moment I turned a major milestone, I started to broadcast it. I am not sure if it was the boldness or security in me that came with that age. People would refer to how I was glowing, and seemed happier. They assumed I was much younger. Experiencing the birth of my grandson and being his care giver has been a great blessing. It has felt like a second chance, like a do over. It has taught me the importance of enjoying and being present in every moment.

Whenever I am out with my grandson, people assume he is my son. It comes as a surprise when I mentioned he is my grandson. Some days I just go along with the assumption, because at the end of the day he is my son. I thank people for their compliments saying "It is the Grace of God" and I thank Him I don't look like what I had been through. God had brought me out of the ashes of the fires that burned in my life. This could only be a testament of His Grace. I had endured a lot through those years. God enabled me to rise up above them all.

A Helpmeet

During the twenty years since God changed my life He has kept me as a single woman. No one has ever asked me out for even a cup of tea. I have gotten looks, but that was about it. I have never thought I should "date" unless I know the person is going to be my husband. I don't think I should go from one guy to the next. That is not for me, and that is what I instilled into my daughter. It was my old lifestyle. When the right person came into my life we would be "courting" not "dating", there is a difference. Through the years, I did wonder why no one came my way or showed any interest? Then I would settle in myself that it must not be the right time for me. I wasn't ready for a relationship or marriage. I also discovered God has set me apart. He has covered and protected me. I once heard someone say "If some people had gotten married at the time they had desired, maybe they would have been divorced not too long after, because it wasn't their time". The timing was off. Have I experienced loneliness? Sure! Do I want to get married? Sure! At this moment I am happy being single. I am not saying that there weren't times through the years I didn't wish I had that special someone by my side to share life with. I knew it wasn't for me to go looking for him. At times I did wish I had someone else making decisions for me. The moment only lasted briefly. I believe and have faith in God and His ability and capability to connect me with someone who is the best person for me. Nothing is impossible for Him. Some people struggle with allowing God to choose their mate. They want him to be hands on for everything else in their lives except choosing their husband or wife. He can touch anything else, except their relationship. I thought if there was anything I wanted God's hands on; it would be choosing my life partner. He is God! He created both of us. Why not wait for God's leading, guidance and direction; He knows who is best suited for me.

There were times I would be encouraged by different individuals to go places to be "seen" and get a husband. I would say "I don't need to do that" I didn't need to go looking for a husband. I believe the scripture in the Bible which states "He who finds a wife finds a good thing, and obtains favor from the Lord" (Proverbs 18:22 NKJV) Well, I want my husband to have favor with God. I believe God is able to bring a husband from China to find me if He sees fit. The person He has chosen and hand-picked according to His desire for me. There are no coincidences with God! He is able to place me in the right place at the right time for the right connection. I believe as I continue to be of service to God and others, His blessings will overflow in my life. I don't think they were convinced of my outlook on the subject.

I have seen too many relationships over the years crumble. I had to wonder if God was their matchmaker or if it was their lack of commitment to each other and the relationship brought it to an end.

It's only been recently that I have allowed an exchange of a hug from anyone from the opposite sex, except from a family member or those I knew had no bad intentions. I didn't want any males to touch me and I mistrusted their motive for hugging me. I am free to allow my instinct to work for me in this area of my life, and to feel out those who are genuine and those who are not.

All this to say there is a God, and He controls time. He can turn back the hands of time enabling us to have a different experience in our life than what we had before. No matter how disastrous we may think it is. With His help we can experience life the way He intended. A life, which is far greater than anything we could imagine. I am happy to freely release the things I can't control in my life to Him. It's more important to me what God does in me, and my life than the promises that I am waiting for Him to fulfill.

Jesus 24/7

One of the things I love about Jesus is His accessibility 24/7. You don't need to make an appointment with Him. I am grateful for the relationship I now have with Him. He is my Prince, my best friend, the lover of my heart, and great rescuer of my soul. He makes me enjoy my salvation. He is my compass. He orders my steps day by day, and is routing for me from Heaven. Letting me know I will make it.

I got to know more about Jesus by spending time in communion and fellowship, with Him. I have learned to listen to Him while He speaks, and in return speak to Him along with observing His ways of working. It has to be a two way street. By doing these things He has made me to be stronger and has given me the ability to strengthen others.

There is a story I heard about a little boy who got himself in trouble with his mom, as little boys often do. He was firmly told to sit down and to be quiet. The little fellow had a stubborn streak and flatly refused. His mother became even more firm and told him to sit down before he got into more trouble than he was already in. Reluctantly, he plopped down in the chair and declared, "Ok, on the outside I'm sitting down, but in the inside I'm still standing up!" I love this story.

Looking back over my transformation, I now see how those times I felt bent over or down for the count as a boxer in the ring, that Jesus was standing up on the inside of me. God had placed a fighting spirit within me. Whenever I went down I always came back up time and time again. I did complain and ask God why I seemed to be fighting all the time. Now I know it was to train, strengthen, and make me stronger like a soldier or any athlete having to work out to bring out the best in them. It was to build my character, and spiritual muscles.

God has invested so much in me. He has certainly called me, and chosen me for such a time as this. His favour is overflowing in my life. Every day I am grateful for His love and His awesome Presence in my life. He has never ever failed me. I know the next stage of my life will be great. I have been called to greatness!

God is able to give joy in time of sorrow, peace in time of confusion, strength and power in time of weakness. The Good News of Salvation is God's ability to accept us just the way we are and turn our life completely around. He will never turn His back on those who believe and call upon Him.

One day, a few years after I was rescued from the life I was living, I met two ladies, from another church. They were visiting our church. I was having a conversation with them and the focus shifted to me. One of the ladies said to the other that I was a woman of worth. That moment was tremendously uplifting for me. Because of the life I had lived, I felt unworthy and at times worthless, without any ambition. After the changes God made in me and my life, I no longer felt that way about myself. I knew I was worthy and created for a purpose. I was the apple of God's eyes. When you know your worth to God, and how precious you are to Him, you see yourself differently and your outlook on life changes. Discovering this truth was a journey for me. I am grateful that God enabled me to weather the storms of my life to get to this discovery. Through it all He has kept me grounded.

Seasons of Change

God is a God of Seasons. His seasonal plan includes periods of growth and periods of rest. Seasons have a beginning and an end. Some seasons are more difficult than others. But every season has a purpose (Ecclesiastes 3:1). As a believer I found out it was necessary for me to be aware of the spiritual seasons, as that of the natural.

While I was in a specific season, it was essential for me to stop and ask myself "What season am I in?" otherwise I would miss the purpose for that particular season. Spring was when I experienced new ministry, opportunities, and fruit bearing. Summer was the experience of spiritual development, fruit bearing, deeper devotion, more awareness of God's Presence, new anointing, and new insight. Autumn was when the greatest harvest came, as a tree heading for its rest; this was a time to return to the essentials of my faith, and new commitment. Winter was the most uncomfortable. I felt as though I was in the wilderness, that God wasn't hearing my prayers and my ministry was unfruitful or dying. It was also a time to reflect on God's faithfulness and a time of rest.

The most important thing I learned while going through my seasons was to get close to God, and to be in touch with Him. I learned that my attitude and the way I responded to my seasons would determine how my spiritual growth would continue, and whether or not I would bear Godly fruits. The seasons were where I received revelations, insights, and truth. It was during these seasons I learned the importance of knowing what God was saying to me, and what He was bringing to pass. It was during these times I learned and matured.

Spiritual growth is a process that has to be gradual. It takes a long time after a seed is sown into the ground before any fruit will appear. Seeds are not bearers of fruits; however they can produce trees that are fruit bearing if the condition and atmosphere are right.

A small plant cannot bear fruit. The weight of the fruit would be very difficult for the plant to handle, therefore causing the plant to collapse and die. Fruits are in a fit condition at a particular time in nature (Mat 21:34). If the fruit is removed before the process of growth is completed it would damage what wasn't able to withstand the ordeal of time. In order for growth and maturity to take place within the fruit it has to go through the process to be perfected. With God there are no alternative routes (1 Tim 3:6).

I am in a new season of my life now. I am excited thinking about all the possibilities that are waiting for me, and to see what God's plans are. I want to go all the way to see what the end will be. I know that He has great things in store for my life. He has brought me this far for His great purpose.

There is so much I want to do, to be, to experience with Jesus in my life. I have been called to prosper, and succeed. I know I will! God's purpose for my life shall come to pass. His Word can't return unto Him void. It has to accomplish what He has sent it to do (Isaiah 55:11). I know He will use my life to be a blessing to others. I want to be like a lighthouse that guides ships into shore on a stormy dark night. He has called me to a powerful charged ministry. I shall do great exploits for Him.

When looking back over those times I used to go to the restaurant in Hull, and the types of people who hung out there, the people who society frowns upon, now I know we were the exact people Jesus died for on the cross. We were the ones He had on His mind. (Mark 2:16-17)

One day while I was driving, as I was approaching an intersection I saw a familiar face. It was a dancer I used to work with in the clubs. She was panhandling. I saw the look on her face; that life had taken its toll. I knew she had been indulging in drugs or alcohol. She looked rough. I was sad to see her in that state. My heart went out to her. I knew at that moment it could have been me in her position. I had to keep moving because the traffic started to move again. It was a busy intersection. I had hoped to see her again but our paths have never crossed again.

My heart's desire and passion is to help those who have travelled the same road I did such as: strippers, prostitutes, homeless, alcoholics, drug addicts, and the ones who have been violated sexually. I desire to bring hope and beauty for ashes to those who can't see any for their future. I know all that I have experienced in my life will not be wasted.

I look forward to seeing what Jesus is going to write in my new story. What a blessing to have Him write me a new story. I know it will be great! People would say my best is yet to come, but I say I am living in my best right now.

It is one thing to hear about God. It is another thing to experience Him for yourself. My life is living proof that God is a God of restoration, second chances, grace, forgiveness, patience, mercy and love.

God's Love

I didn't always feel this way during the times of my first walk with God. I struggled with the concept that He really loved me Elaine, as an individual. I didn't trust Him. Because of my experiences in my life I saw Him as a dictator. Someone I couldn't please. For a period of time, my prayer always was for God to help me to feel the love people told me He had for me. I couldn't feel it. I asked Him to help me to open up my heart to receive it. I was in desperate need of it, and in return I would be able to give it back to Him and others.

After crying out to God, I saw how He answered my prayers through my circumstances and situations. He showed me I could trust Him. I had to make up my mind that I believed Him. I opened up my heart to Him and embraced His love. I kept thinking about what I read in the Bible where it said "Without faith it is impossible to please God." (Hebrews 11:6) After I made the decision to believe He really loved me, I felt at peace. I started to experience an unexplainable reality of God in my life. I now feel an overflowing of abundance of His love for me (Romans 5:5). The love of God is amazing. It is deeper than any ocean, wider than any sea, higher than any mountain, stronger than any chains, or bondages that tries to keep me bound. God's love has no limits or boundaries. Because of God's love the self loathing and insecurities have been replaced with learning to love and appreciate myself each day. My lack of confidence is no longer an issue. The more I place confidence in Him, the more He releases His confidence in me to be myself. I have been forever changed, because of God's love for me. It really is a good feeling to love and be loved; to do good unto others and have the same returned unto you without any expectation.

One of the things I appreciate and respect about God is the free will (which He has given to us as His creative beings) to make choices. We have the choice to do whatever we want to do. But as a parent gives instructions on what to do and what not to do, so it is with God. There is a consequence that comes with every choice and decision we make and rightly so. There is a price to pay for disobedience. It says in the Bible "Whatever a man sows he shall reap" (Galatians 6:7), some people say what goes around comes around. Getting to know Jesus and having Him in my life has helped me to discover what I really desire. I choose to surrender my life to Him, and to allow Him to make me into the best person I can be. My choice is to have Him help me to have the best that this life can offer. Doing what I know He expects of me.

I don't believe you can believe in God and not believe in the existence of Satan (devil). I don't believe you can believe in Heaven and not believe in Hell. I don't believe you can believe in good and not believe in evil. God represents light and Satan represents darkness. If you haven't experienced the depth of the darkness of this life, you will not be able to be grateful and fully appreciate the light of salvation.

My life experiences has proven that there is a God of love who loves me, and a devil who is evil and tried to help me destroy myself and my life with drugs and alcohol. He tried to keep me in a place of darkness, where there was no light or hope. I know there is a Heaven, and with God's help I will get to see it one day after I have fulfilled my purpose and destiny. Each day, He gives me the courage to keep walking by faith to follow Him and His calling upon my life. I am trusting in Him fully that He will do it.

God is real. No one can prove to me otherwise. I have experienced Him for myself and still experiencing Him each day. Amazing Grace how sweet the sound, that came and rescued me. Jesus is my Prince, my King. He is many things all rolled up in one. Before I cried out for help and Jesus heard me, I used to hope that someone would come and rescue me like the prince rescued the damsel in distress in the fairy tales. Deep down inside I knew I needed to be rescued from myself. I had no hope for a better life before I met Jesus, but now I walk in hope. Surrendering my life to Him has set me free. He has brought order into my life. Now I can see, after what seemed like a long time of things looking bleak and murky. I couldn't see the big picture before, but now I can see myself. I can see the woman God has brought out from within me; after all I have been through. I have learned to endure great pain, but still persevere. He has endowed me with great power and authority. Only He could have brought me through the process, and it was for my good!

I didn't understand the process of transformation that was needed. My perception along the way had to be changed. Healing of the mind, the heart and the soul had to take place. God changes us on the inside to enable us to deal with our outward circumstances, but our preference would be for Him to change our circumstances on the outside to accommodate us, which usually will never be the case.

I know He has a great work for me to do in His Kingdom. It was necessary for me to go through all those tough experiences to facilitate my effectiveness to where He is bringing me. I am called and already equipped for such a time as this to do whatever the master bids me to do. I will not be defeated because He is with me.

I am preordained; predestined to win. I had to keep getting back up. He lifted me up in the fullness of time, and by the great power of His Name. After all my life altering experiences that could've stopped me in my tracks, I am still standing! Out of the ashes I arise! God has given me beauty for ashes! With a grateful heart I have to say "Thank you Jesus for being so good to me!" "You are Good and Your Mercy endures forever!" Amen!

She's Still Standing!

We cast her into a lake of fire, expected her to crash, and gave her the worst possible attack

We troubled her on every side, but she's still standing, we tried to contain her but she's still expanding

We denied her promotion, but she's still marching forward just making progress

We hit her with the worst possible blow, but she's still standing and moving forward because the Pillar of fire showed up!

Dr. Ralph Dartey

Some of My Favourite Songs

He lives	– Alan Jackson
Lord prepare me to be a sanctuary	– Authors Randy Scruggs and John W. Thompson
I am available to you	– Rev. Milton Brunson
Beauty for Ashes	– Tye Tribbett
Alabaster Box	– CeCe Winans
Fill my cup, Lord	– CeCe Winians
Mercy said no	– CeCe Winians
The Blood that Will Never Lose Its Power	– Andrae Crouch
My testimony	– Marvin Sapp
Never would have made it	– Marvin Sapp
In The Garden	– Marvin Sapp
I know who I am	– Sinach
I Rejoice	– Sinach
I am not alone	– Kari Jobe
Overcomer	– Mandisa

Stronger	– Mandisa
Alive	– Hillsong Young & Free
He'll do it again	– Shirley Caesar
I give myself away	– William McDowell
I smile	– Kirk Franklin
In Christ alone	– Newboys
In your presence	– Juanita Bynum
Jesus at the centre of it all	– Israel Houghton & New Breed
Deeper	– Isarel Houghton & New Breed
Oceans	– Hillsong United
Still	– Hillsong
Victories Crown	– Darlene Zschech
In Jesus Name	– Darlene Zschech
Take me to the King	– Tamela Mann
With you	– James Fortune & FIYA
Hold on	– Fred Hammond, James Fortune & FIYA
10,000 Reasons	– Jesus Culture & Kim Walker
You are my strength	– William Murphy
Can't live a day without you	– Avalon
Jesus is my help	– Hezekiah Walker
Faithful is our God	– Hezekiah Walker & LFC
Every Praise	– Hezekiah Walker
I Almost Let Go	– Kurt Carr

Some of My Favourite Scriptures

Deuteronomy 28

Joshua 1

Job 38, 39, 40, 41, 42

Psalms 3, 23, 24, 27, 37, 6, 62, 91, 105, 116, 121, 124, 126, 138, 139, 145

Proverbs 3

Isaiah 40, 43, 54, 55, 61

Ezekiel 37

Daniel 3, 7

Jeremiah 29

Matthew 13

Luke 15

John 4, 10, 14, 15

Romans 8, 12

I Corinthians 2, 13

II Corinthians 5

Galatians 2, 4

Ephesians 3, 6

Philippians 4

Colossians 1, 3

II Timothy 4

Hebrews 11, 12

CPSIA information can be obtained
at www.ICGtesting.com
Printed in the USA
LVOW03s0251300917
550598LV00008B/8/P